How to Have **ANTIRACIST
CONVERSATIONS**

HOW TO HAVE ANTI RACIST CONVERSATIONS

EMBRACING OUR FULL HUMANITY TO CHALLENGE WHITE SUPREMACY

ROXY MANNING, PhD

Berrett–Koehler Publishers, Inc.

Berrett-Koehler Publishers, Inc.
1333 Broadway, Suite 1000
Oakland, CA 94612-1921
Tel: (510) 817-2277
Fax: (510) 817-2278
www.bkconnection.com

ORDERING INFORMATION

QUANTITY SALES. Special discounts are available on quantity purchases by corporations, associations, and others. For details, contact the "Special Sales Department" at the Berrett-Koehler address above.

INDIVIDUAL SALES. Berrett-Koehler publications are available through most bookstores. They can also be ordered directly from Berrett-Koehler: Tel: (800) 929-2929; Fax: (802) 864-7626; www.bkconnection.com.

ORDERS FOR COLLEGE TEXTBOOK / COURSE ADOPTION USE. Please contact Berrett-Koehler: Tel: (800) 929-2929; Fax: (802) 864-7626.

Distributed to the US trade and internationally by Penguin Random House Publisher Services.

Berrett-Koehler and the BK logo are registered trademarks of Berrett-Koehler Publishers, Inc.

Printed in the United States of America

Berrett-Koehler books are printed on long-lasting acid-free paper. When it is available, we choose paper that has been manufactured by environmentally responsible processes. These may include using trees grown in sustainable forests, incorporating recycled paper, minimizing chlorine in bleaching, or recycling the energy produced at the paper mill.

Library of Congress Cataloging-in-Publication Data
    Names: Manning, Roxy, author.
    Title: How to have antiracist conversations : embracing our full humanity to challenge white supremacy / Roxy Manning, PhD.
    Description: First edition. | Oakland, CA : Berrett-Koehler Publishers, [2023] | Includes bibliographical references and index.
    Identifiers: LCCN 2023006194 (print) | LCCN 2023006195 (ebook) | ISBN 9781523003730 (paperback ; alk. paper) | ISBN 9781523003747 (pdf) | ISBN 9781523003754 (epub) | ISBN 9781523003761 (audio)
    Subjects: LCSH: Antiracism. | Racism. | Nonviolence. | Race relations.
    Classification: LCC HT1563 .M2363 2023 (print) | LCC HT1563 (ebook) | DDC 305.8—dc23/eng/20230313
    LC record available at https://lccn.loc.gov/2023006194
    LC ebook record available at https://lccn.loc.gov/2023006195

First Edition

31 30 29 28 27 26 25 24 23 | 10 9 8 7 6 5 4 3 2 1

Book producer and designer: BookMatters
Cover designer: Susan Malikowski, DesignLeaf Studio
Cover illustration: Mireille van Bremen (The Visual Mediator) and Roxy Manning
Author photo: Matt Wong

For my parents, Lois and Milton,

and all the parents who dream of a better future

For my children, Theodore, Anika, and Micah,

and all the children for whom we dream

For all who work for Beloved Community

CONTENTS

FOREWORD

I am honored to offer these words in celebration of Dr. Roxy Manning's years of dedicated effort, modeling, and teaching that have led to the book you hold in your hands. As a friend, former colleague, and occasional collaborator of Dr. Manning, I notice what in Buddhism is called *mudita*, or vicarious joy, picturing people of all races benefiting from this beautiful effort. As a practitioner of nonviolence, restorative justice, and antiracism, I rejoice in the support you will receive, especially at work and in community life.

Group work is necessary. Group work can be especially powerful when the lived experiences of members differ significantly from one another. It can take you places. The better you are at navigating and working together, the more adventures you can go on. In the best case scenario, group work can bring you into what Dr. Martin Luther King Jr. called Beloved Community. Beloved Community offers a sense of dynamic belonging. It's a vision of a world or society or even a circle of coworkers where everyone knows they matter and are valued. It is not without conflict, divergence, or differences. Beloved Community arises when we value one another and resolve conflicts with respect. Trust builds, and trust is perhaps the major protective factor in and ingredient for transformational work.

I have had the privilege of time with Dr. Manning in numerous settings for more than fifteen years. As you will discover, she communicates, and teaches others to communicate, with surgical precision and with empathy. In this book, as she has done in hundreds of workshops and retreats, Dr. Manning offers specific support to Global Majority people to speak their truth. She offers coaching and concrete strategies throughout. She models through sharing stories of her lived experiences that are painful to read for their impact and important to share for all of us on the collective journey of learning to transform, rather than transmit, harm.

Dr. Manning extends new skills to white people like me who were not raised to understand, or even perceive, the grinding, systemic harm of racism. For white readers this book will expand capacity in communication, in conflicts, and in holding systems perspectives. The approaches she shares offer ways to dissolve the shame that blocks action. These capacities matter, as many times I have observed white individuals, including leaders at every level, enact this dynamic: "What often amazes me about white folks—including myself—is how easily we become paralyzed when it comes to anti-racism work. In almost every other area of life, if we faced some kind of problem, we'd talk to others and make a plan to try to address it. In anti-racism work, however, we seem to freeze and get easily confused. Yet so much is available to us."*

*M. Boucher, "Behavior Modification Experiments in Resisting White Supremacy in Clinical Practice," in K. Hardy, ed., *The Enduring, Invisible and Ubiquitous Centrality of Whiteness* (New York: W. W. Norton & Co., 2022), 499.

Dr. Manning's work is an important resource now available to all of us. Keep it close, as a blueprint for co-creating a world that works for all.

—Kit Miller, Director Emerit
  M.K. Gandhi Institute for Nonviolence

Introduction

You've picked up a book that has already sparked debate. "Why talk about being 'antiracist'?" asked some liberal (often white) people when they learned of the topic. "Instead of talking about what we *don't* want—racism—we should be talking about what we *do* want—a just, equitable world where everyone can thrive." And some of my activist friends (often those who identify as part of the Global Majority) also protested.[1] "How can you talk about Beloved Community and shared human needs in the face of outright racism and inequity?" they asked. They worried the focus on reaching for our shared humanity was just another way of saying, "I don't see race—we're all human." This line of race-blind thinking, another form of racism, harmfully sidelines the specific needs, concerns, and experiences of Global Majority people.

As I listened to these concerns, I gained more clarity about why I needed to write this book. At one point or another in my own journey, I agreed fully with each of these positions. Indeed, I still do to some extent. I'm a Black Caribbean immigrant. I'm aware (now) that my experience as an immigrant reflects just one slice of the many ways that the belief in white supremacy has impacted Black people cross the diaspora. My understanding of race has necessarily been impacted by my identity. Yet even as I come from a country where Black people were also enslaved and seen as second-class citizens for so long, our experience was different than the experience of Black people in the United States.

In my country, for example, the first prime minister after independence from Britain was a Black man, forty-seven years before the United States had a Black head of state. One can infer from that simple fact the vastly different opportunities and sense of possibility Black people in most countries across the diaspora might experience, compared with those in the United States. When I came to the United States, I had that sense of hope, of endless possibility. After all, my parents chose to emigrate here because of the belief that the educational and vocational opportunities that would be available to their children would be limitless. I can't imagine many Black Americans at the time (let alone today) held that view.

Seven years old when I arrived in the United States, I began to engage with the complexities of race in the United States and how I fit in as Black immigrant only after many years. As a child living in Harlem, New York, I attended some schools where Black people were 95 percent of the student population and others where Black people were about 5 percent. Throughout my entire educational career, I told myself, "I don't know how to fit in. I'm too Caribbean for the US-born Black students at my elementary school, and too Black *and* too Caribbean for the white and Asian students at my middle and high schools." I always assumed there was something I should be doing differently to fit in. Each time I experienced discrimination, exclusion, and outright racism, I felt that it must have been my own fault.

Since I couldn't see how cultural racism was impacting me, I couldn't free myself from the responsibility I felt to fully embody the American Dream. It was the land of opportunity, wasn't it, with advancement limited only by my effort and persistence. I, like all the immigrants I met, trusted that narrative, not seeing how it was steeped in the values of white supremacy culture. I worried that my failures would be seen as further proof of the inferiority of Black people. You can imagine my surprise, my outrage, my despair, when I finally began to have a glimmer of this larger force—a belief in white supremacy—and how it shapes all our lives. The emergence of white supremacy as a cultural belief system was driven by capitalistic motivations to elevate whiteness in order to justify the exploitation and enslavement of the lands and people in the Americas—Indigenous/First Nation peoples and people of African descent forcibly brought from their land—and of Indigenous people and their lands worldwide.

What could I do with that new knowledge? As an outsider in both communities—the Black Harlem community of my childhood and the white and Asian communities of my adolescence—it was not easy for me to summarily reject one group or the other, as I saw others do. I had found small pockets of friends, all of whom held different identities from me, as I moved through the various communities of my childhood. In elementary school I was befriended by a girl who, having a larger framed body and a mother who was a paraplegic, was also seen as an outsider. In middle and high school I found refuge in four close friends who were also outside the popular crowd—an immigrant from China and one from the Dominican Republic, a white boy who was gay, and a white girl from a fiercely liberal family.

My burgeoning awareness of white supremacy culture as a teenager coincided with my awareness of all the various ways patriarchy and heteronormativity worked to elevate some people and demote others. I wanted to be free of it all, but I also wanted freedom for my friends, since I could see how they too were not served by the systems in which we found ourselves. Relatively early in my life, I began to yearn for a community that embraced us all, one in which we could all thrive, a community that treasured our uniqueness and supported and valued all of us equally. Without yet knowing of the concept as used by Martin Luther King Jr., what I wanted was Beloved Community.

As I entered adulthood, I wrestled with my intersecting identities. Despite doing all the things that society values— earning my PhD, getting married, having children, and so on—I wasn't happy. The more that I achieved, the greater the risk was that someone would decide that I actually *didn't* belong. My harsh self-judgments, which contained many of the toxic messages of white supremacy culture, functioned as the whip that kept me in line and kept me doing the things I was told I should do. But even though I was fine with being my own harshest critic, I knew I didn't want to act that way toward others. So when someone did anything that I perceived as racist or typical of white supremacy culture, I would see-saw wildly between two possible responses: either harshly condemn and shame them (as shame was such an effective motivator for me to change my behavior) or embrace them with empathy and openhearted curiosity (which is the way I so wished that I was responded to). Most times, I ended up silent. I didn't know how to show up and advocate for myself while holding that intention of care and compassion toward the other person. I wanted Beloved Community, but at that time I could only imagine a community that worked for me *or* worked for the other, not one that truly worked for everyone.

In my early thirties, shortly after earning my doctorate in clinical psychology, my dissertation adviser told me about Nonviolent Communication, both as a communication model and a way of thinking about human relations grounded in the belief that all human behavior is motivated by the same universal, essential needs. I had never heard about it. After raving about how much Nonviolent Communication had changed her life, she encouraged me to study it since I was "so disconnected from my needs." My adviser never said how the ideas embedded in Nonviolent Communication would help me, and not knowing what she was talking about, I nodded politely as I thought of all the things I needed to do as a mother of two children under three. When she offered to send me to the very next intensive training on Nonviolent Communication, a training that happened to be in Argentina, I perked up. I was delighted by the possibility of going to Argentina, if only for the break from parenting.

At that Nonviolent Communication training and subsequent ones, things began to click. I realized how much I had indeed learned to prioritize other people's well-being and other people's comfort, no matter the cost to myself. I began to understand how my fierce self-judgment had been an attempt to protect myself from shock by preempting the onslaught of negative messages that were directed my way whenever I deviated from society's expectations. Understanding this allowed me to hold even the cruelest parts of myself with self-compassion and understanding. Soon I was able to start bringing curiosity and compassion to even the aspects of my behavior that caused me the most harm. This work helped me find a way past the dilemma in which I had been stuck: the either/or seesaw of silence I mentioned earlier. I didn't have to choose between myself and other people any longer. Instead, I saw the power and freedom I gained when I identified both my needs and the needs of others, then persevered in dialogues to find new ways of engaging with each other. While a perfect solution could not always be found, I discovered that even the attempt to find solutions helped to heal the wounds of exclusion that so many of us have.

The development of my capacity to compassionately acknowledge what I needed helped me realize that my past emphasis on prioritizing the well-being of others, especially at cost to myself, was a manifestation of white supremacy culture. White supremacy culture values the well-being of white people above that of anyone else. At white supremacy culture's worst manifestation, Black people's lives, well-being, and humanity are completely devalued. Black death, in this cultural system, is acceptable when it benefits white people and white profit. Although the chattel enslavement of Black people that was one goal of the proponents of white supremacy ideology is no longer legal in the United States, the culture and institutions that created this value system still pervade our society today. So many Global Majority people have internalized the message that their path to a safe and comfortable life requires them to accept any indignity and keep white people happy, no matter the cost to themselves. We display this belief in so many ways (e.g., working twice as hard for half as much pay, giving up our culture, and assimilating to keep white people comfortable).

I believed I could only receive acceptance if I stayed silent and always forgave or empathized, even when I had experienced significant harm. Sitting in this revelation of my own behavior, I finally understood why so many Global Majority people so fiercely reject the request to empathize with white people's expressions of shame and guilt. Many people push back against concepts like Beloved Community and Nonviolent Communication, believing it asks us to care for the well-being of people who will never care for ours. When we ourselves are in need, the idea of doing even more labor to care for white people can feel like an untenable continuation of white supremacy culture's rules. *When will we be the ones receiving care? Why is it that a white person's shame gets more attention than a Global Majority person's oppression?*

As much as I resonated with this line of thinking, I also saw the trap within it. White supremacy culture forces us to disregard our very human connection, to see people in categories. It tries to force us into one of two roles—either the perpetual caretaker or the angry protester. Combining the visions of Beloved Community and Nonviolent Communication, however, I hope for a different path. When we reject the either/or dichotomy, showing up with our full power to advocate for our own needs while caring for each person's humanity, determined to exclude no one, we can work together to create truly transformative systems and ways of interacting that enable all our communities to thrive. Nonviolent Communication provides a path to Beloved Community. It enables us to unapologetically name racist harm when it occurs, to persist in advocating for change, in a way that holds care for all.

We do so not from the white supremacy culture imperative to speak and act in ways that keep white people feeling safe and comfortable, but because the change we seek will last longer and will have more people working to make it stick, if we all benefit from it.

Some people find it confusing for me to suggest we speak up about injustice in ways that hold care for everyone, while still using words like "racist," "privilege," "microaggression," or "white supremacy culture." Those words land for some as judgments that are disconnecting and automatically create division. I use these words because I don't see them as judgments. Instead, they are observations—descriptors seeking to define a real phenomenon. Sometimes, by using these words, there is immediate resonance. When I name a behavior as racist to a person of the Global Majority, there is often a shared understanding of what I'm referring to. We can immediately understand that I am using this word, racist, to describe an action that is benefiting members of one racial or ethnic group at the expense of those in other groups. If I were to use that word with someone who didn't share that understanding, we could talk about what they got from my use of that word, and we can, through dialogue, come to a shared agreement of what the word refers to and the meaning.

This is what I mean by speaking fiercely, with care for all. I don't shy from using words that name hard truths, but I also take care that my meaning is understood. If someone tells me, "When I hear you say that my behavior is racist, I hear you say I am a bad person," I can clarify what I wish to convey. I can respond by talking about the differential impact to which I'm drawing attention, what I meant when I say "racist behavior," and I can make clear that I don't assume this speaks to a person's intention or morality. I firmly believe that acknowledging and attempting to address a phenomenon and its impact requires us to name it. We cannot shy away from these topics because of the discomfort that they may cause. Although I agree that when I use a word like "racism" I may create a disconnection with some people, the idea that this is a reason to stop using the word makes no sense to me. That line of reasoning prioritizes some (often white) people's ease in conversation, at the expense of some (often Global Majority) people's trust that their experience is being seen and acknowledged. Seeking to eliminate words that stimulate discomfort is a practice that prioritizes the needs of members of one group over the needs of another group—which is exactly the kind of differential impact that we are seeking to eliminate.

Dr. Marshall B. Rosenberg, founder of Nonviolent Communication, shared in an interview the importance of being able to name challenges and advocate for change in ways that liberate us all. He described the significant learning and collaboration he experienced with two grassroots activists working against racism and sexism, and shared an insight from this collaboration that influenced his work: "Important in this was discovering the causes of oppression and how to liberate oneself and others from it at different levels, both within oneself and socially."[2] Rosenberg went on to celebrate the two activists, stating:

> Vicki and Al were very valuable in helping me see the complex interconnections between the personal and the social. They were rare people who saw how to connect the political and the personal and the spiritual. They had

the structural analysis. They can show you how the system is oppressive. They know how it works. I learned parts of this from other people, too. But some people—because they didn't have things integrated—weren't as committed to personal growth. They would preach political stuff, but they'd oppress people. There were very few people...who really had it together. But I was fortunate enough to be working with a lot of them.[3]

In writing *Antiracist Conversations* and developing the Authentic Dialogue framework I present within this book, I aspire to do what Dr. Rosenberg described: to bring together the complex intersections between the personal and the social. It is grounded in my years of work with numerous colleagues, both Global Majority people and white people, who have labored to use the principles of Nonviolent Communication to support antiracist work. My hope is that while you're reading this book, the term "antiracist" makes sense and aligns fully with your purpose. "Antiracist" speaks to our current efforts to name and dismantle the racism that permeates societies throughout the world. And when we succeed, when we finally establish Beloved Community, the word "antiracist" will be an anachronistic curiosity in a world without racism.

Heavily grounded in the tenets of Nonviolent Communication and Beloved Community, the Authentic Dialogue framework you will learn weaves together an explicit attention to addressing inequitable systems and political structures with a commitment to the establishment of Beloved Community, one in which resources are shared by all to enable our individual and collective thriving. The model grounds us in that consciousness and uses the principles and tools of Nonviolent

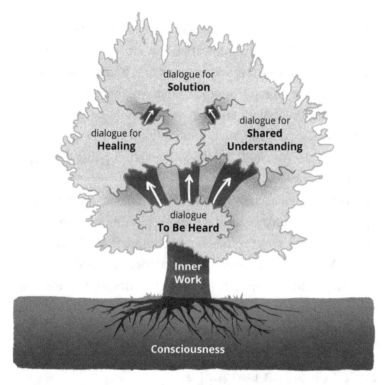

FIGURE 1. **Map of Authentic Dialogue**
© Mireille van Bremen and Roxy Manning

Communication to support our ability to have tough conversations that help to dismantle oppressive social structures such as racism. As you read this book, you'll learn about the inner work that supports engaging in Authentic Dialogue and explore the four types of dialogues shown in Figure 1.

For those people who are already engaged in nonviolent action or political action, the Authentic Dialogue framework can be a guide for how to have important conversations when everyone is finally in the room, ready to talk. It teaches us how to name harm as it is happening, surface what is important to all involved, and identify strategies that are truly equitable and antiracist. For those people who are committed to Nonviolent Communication but are uncertain how to use it to address systemic inequities and harm in ways that don't continue to replicate the underlying beliefs that drive such harm, this book can support you in going beyond interpersonal dialogues that implicitly assume everyone is on a level playing field. I go beyond exploring just the steps of Nonviolent Communication, because I have seen all too often how, when used by themselves without an awareness of oppressive structures and how they operate intrapersonally and interpersonally, the steps can continue to reinforce inequities. As part of this, we explore the underlying belief system that shapes both Nonviolent Communication and antiracism work to build Beloved Community so that we can more intentionally align our behaviors with our values.

Let's Talk about Language

As you read this book, you'll come across a number of terms that I am deliberately choosing to use. A key one is the difference between "a dialogue" and "a conversation." I think of a conversation as any exchange between people in which information is shared. Conversations can have several purposes. They can be functional, in which we focus on exchanging information accurately. They can be healing, focusing on soothing someone's pain. They can be strategic, aimed at achieving a shared goal. Dialogues, the focus of this book, are a very specific kind of conversation. While all dialogues are inherently conversations, not all conversations are dialogues. When I speak of Authentic Dialogues, I speak of an exchange in which we seek to understand someone's true experience—how they feel, what's important to them, what they need—as well as to make our own experience known to them. In this encounter we are each open to being changed by the other. Like all conversations, dialogues can be unidirectional (one can join with the intention of understanding another person's experience) or multidirectional (all parties hold an intention to share vulnerably and to understand the others). In general, when we say "conversation" in this book, we are referring to a specific type of conversation—Authentic Dialogues.

I want to clarify another set of terms. Since we are talking about racism and its impact, we reference Actors (people who do racist acts), Receivers (people who experience racist acts), and Bystanders (people who witness racist acts). This terminology is grounded in the work of Dominic Barter, who stewarded the development and utilization of Restorative Circles as a conflict resolution practice within Brazil and worldwide.[4] It avoids the language of "victim" and "perpetrator" because these labels of "perpetrator" and "victim" are more than just descriptive words letting us know who did what. They are also often laden with judgments and values. When you think of "victim," you might envision someone who is weak and vulnerable, a good person in pain who needs protection. When you think of "perpetrator," you might envision someone who is strong, bad, uncaring—a person from whom we must protect others. The words shift us from descriptions of who was impacted in a situation or who caused impact to static judgments about each person's role in a situation. The "perpetrator" not only did something that had an unwanted impact, they were also a bad person. The "victim" is no longer simply someone who was impacted by someone else's actions, but also someone who is weak and needs protection.

Barter suggests using language that reduces our tendency to conjure up these static judgments, however unconsciously, while we engage in the necessary dialogue to acknowledge and repair the harm. When I can see you as a person who did something that resulted in harm without seeing you as an essentially evil person, I am more likely to advocate for strategies that include your well-being in the repair that is being sought. When I see you as a person who experienced harm without seeing you as weak, I'm more likely to center your voice and preferences in solutions that are empowering instead of taking a paternalistic caretaking stance that continues to disempower you. The words Actor and Receiver remove judgment—an Actor can take an action that results in harm or one that results in benefit, and the Receiver can experience the action as harmful or supportive. The words Actor and Receiver make clear the relationship between two people in a way that preserves our capacity to hold each person's full humanity and the complexity of what they bring to any situation.

The Bystander role is also important in this book. Bystanders may witness an act happening but not be the object of the act themselves. Bystanders can be impacted by what they witnessed even if they were not the focus of the act. In fact, one aim of many nonviolent actions has been to mobilize folks initially into the Bystander role—to get people who are not direct targets of unjust laws or violence and who may even be unaware of them to notice what is happening. And in noticing, to be impacted and moved to intervene. Bystanders who were forced to witness the cruelty and indignities of injustices throughout history have been instrumental in speaking up to protest those policies that did not align with their vision of the world in which they wanted to live.

It's important to emphasize that I don't believe these are the only words that can describe these relationships, or the only ways we can discuss without judgment those who are impacted and those who impact. It's all too easy to focus on whether someone is using the "right" language and lose track of the intention, which is to talk about these interactions in ways that help free us from the right-wrong dualistic thinking that continues to separate us. I invite you to use whatever language works for you and your community while holding on to the intention to bring a needs-based assessment, rather than a moralistic one, to these issues.

You have likely noticed another phrase I use that is not yet commonly used—people of the Global Majority. As defined by Rosemary Campbell-Stephens, "the term 'Global Majority' includes those people who identify as Black, African, Asian, Brown, Arab and mixed heritage, are indigenous to the global south, and/or have been racialized as 'ethnic minorities.'"[5] Campbell-Stephens asserts that when we use the word "minority" to describe folks of the Global Majority, we linguistically obscure the fact that this group is actually much larger in terms of population size than the group containing people of European heritage, which she notes is approximately 85 percent to 15 percent respectively.[6] Using a phrase like "ethnic minority" logically sets us up to contrast "minority" with a group that must therefore be the majority—another subtle reinforcement of beliefs stemming from white supremacy culture. I prefer this term as it moves us away from identifying people using inaccurate terms such as "people of color" (Isn't white a color? Am I Black if my skin tone is light enough for me to pass as white?) or "nonwhite" (which sets whiteness as the norm and others in contrast to it). There will be times when I quote someone who might use a different phrase or terminology. I choose to honor each person's choice about how they self-identify and retain their original language.

Throughout this book I share many interactions that I have had with people as well as some sample dialogues. Any example that includes me is shared as accurately as I can recall. While I cannot remember verbatim every word that's been spoken in each exchange, I make sure to share the essence of what I remember and the language that I or others may have used. When the person was available, I shared what I wrote about them and checked with them for accuracy. It is important to note that any person referred to by name in a dialogue or scenario is referenced pseudonymously. I, or the Receiver, chose names that were consistent with the ethnic background of anyone named but did not use the actual name of the Actor or Receiver. In all but one sample dialogue in the book, the actual Receiver in the dialogue engaged in the practice dialogue, which is written in their words. Either another person or I role-played the Actor. The purpose of this was twofold: the role-playing served as a check of accuracy of my description of the original event and gave the Receiver an opportunity to revisit an Act that had been a source of pain for them. Many reported that the opportunity to redo the dialogue, with me or another person role-playing the Actor, was healing for them.

What You'll Learn

Now that I've shared some information to orient you to the language used throughout the book, let's jump in. In the next few chapters we establish a shared understanding about the values underlying this work and what I mean by Beloved Community. We'll explore what gets in the way of us living these values—what white supremacy culture is and how it interacts with our brain's very functioning to make it challenging for us to be antiracist, despite our best intentions.

Once we're clear on how we want to move through the world and what gets in the way, we'll explore some concepts of Nonviolent Communication that can be supportive, then situate them within the Authentic Dialogue framework. Along the way you'll learn a little bit more about me, and you'll get to see some examples of Authentic Dialogues in practice, especially in relation to responding to microaggressions. If you would like to dive more deeply into these concepts and to discover and clear the roots of any discomfort that you feel about reaching for Beloved Community, I invite you to explore the framework of Authentic Dialogue and the neuroscience of self-compassion with the help of the companion handbook, *The Antiracist Heart: A Self-Compassion and Activism Handbook*, written by me and my friend Sarah Peyton.[7]

NOTES

1. The term Global Majority "includes those people who identify as Black, African, Asian, Brown, Arab and mixed heritage, are indigenous to the global south, and/or have been racialized as 'ethnic minorities.'" Rosemary M. Campbell-Stephens, *Educational Leadership and the Global Majority: Decolonising Narratives* (Cham, Switzerland: Springer Nature, 2021), 7.

2. Quoted in Marjorie Cross Witty, "Marshall Rosenberg," chapter 7 in "Life History Studies of Committed Lives (Volumes I–III)," PhD dissertation, Northwestern University, 1990, pp. 778-779.

3. Quoted in Witty, "Marshall Rosenberg," 785-786.

4. Dominic Barter, "Introduction to Restorative Circles," workshop presented at the New York Intensive in Nonviolent Communication, Albany, NY, August 5, 2008.

5. Campbell-Stephens, *Educational Leadership*, 7.

6. Campbell-Stephens, *Educational Leadership*, 7.

7. Roxy Manning and Sarah Peyton, *The Antiracist Heart: A Self-Compassion and Activism Handbook* (Oakland, CA: Berrett-Koehler, 2023).

1

What's the Point? Dialogue for Beloved Community

When I was in my early twenties, I was in a car traveling on Highway 17 in New York, on my way to visit my boyfriend who lived in upstate New York. A friend was driving. We were having the kind of earnest conversations that twenty-year-olds have, letting our minds wander along with our hearts. My brother slept in the back seat, leaning against the window. The dark night and blurry scenery wove a cozy cocoon where we could all relax, enjoying each other's company.

My friend and I were startled out of our cozy warmth when flashing lights jolted into view. A police car had pulled up behind us, following us. *Did it want us to pull over?* We looked at the speedometer—we were driving just a mile above the speed limit. We nervously pulled over onto the side of the road. The lights and sudden shift in movement had jostled my sleeping brother, and I heard him groggily attempt to make sense of what was going on. "Are we there already?" he asked sleepily, from the back seat. The officer tapped on the window before we were able to answer my brother. My friend rolled the window down and instead of receiving the usual request for license and registration, he was asked to step out of the car. The officer had his hand resting on his gun. They walked together out of earshot of the car. My brother and I sat in the car, confused and anxious, unable to make sense of what was happening. We watched the officer and my friend talk, at first with visible tension in their bodies. After a few minutes, I saw the tension slowly dissipate—the officer's hand slid off his gun, his shoulders dropped, his posture relaxed.

My friend walked back to our car while the officer walked to his. I was even more confused. When my friend got back in the car, he sat quietly for a little while. The police car drove away, and then my friend started the car and we got back on the road. My brother and I kept asking him about what had happened, but he seemed reluctant to tell us. Finally, he spoke. But I could tell, as he was speaking, that he was wishing that what he was saying wasn't real. "The officer saw us passing him on the road. He saw me—a white man—in the driver's seat, and you next to me, a Black person. And he saw your brother in the back seat. He wanted to make sure I wasn't being kidnapped."

None of us knew what to say. I felt a rush of anger in my body: like a slap. Before I could really feel the anger, it became shame. Hot and overwhelming. I felt as though this officer's racism meant I had done something wrong. I could tell my brother was vibrating with anger, but he didn't know how to navigate what had happened either. We were all silent. We didn't talk anymore about it, we turned the radio on and finished the drive in silence. This officer, who had seen Black folks and white folks driving together, couldn't conceive of us as being part of the same Beloved Community.

After that incident I avoided any interaction with the police. Several years later, I was driving in a rural area, this time alone, again at night. As I took an exit ramp, I switched lanes on the ramp to make the left turn I knew was coming. Again, those flashing lights appeared in my rearview mirror. I was terrified. I took out my phone and called 911, telling the operator that I was being pulled over and was going to drive to a gas station so that I could stop in a well-lit place. As I drove three minutes to reach a gas station, I started trembling. By the time I parked and the officer approached me, I was shaking and crying, tears streaming down my face, taking hiccupy breaths. I didn't know what PTSD was at the time, so I didn't know how to soothe my dysregulated body. I felt so exposed, so unsafe. The young, white police officer at my window looked alarmed when he saw me.

"What's wrong," he asked.

"Nothing," I stammered. He looked even more perturbed. "Do you have a weapon? Are there drugs in the car?"

"No," I said, tears streaming heavily.

The officer kept trying, confusedly, to reassure me. "You'll be fine. Everything's fine." I continued to cry as he explained, "I pulled you over because you switched lanes on the ramp. You're not supposed to do that." He left without giving me a ticket. I sat in the brightly lit gas station, shaking and crying. In that moment I realized what was terrifying: I did not believe that this officer would see me, see my humanity. That he would see me as part of his Beloved Community, someone deserving of care. I was convinced he would see me as a threat, an outcast from his community, so that my life was in danger from his traffic stop.

As I write this, I hold so much compassion for each person in these situations. My white friend, who did not know how to respond when racism thrust itself into his sedate life. My brother and me, being reminded once again that even when we're doing nothing at all—sleeping, chatting, riding in a car—someone who does not see us as part of their Beloved Community will make assumptions about us that could have had much worse outcomes. My traumatized self, being conditioned to not only believe that a white police officer would not see me as a person worth protecting, but that there was no way either of us could see each other as part of Beloved Community. And the officer, faced with a visibly scared Black woman with no clue of how to make things better.

I wanted to write this book because the idea of Beloved Community—a world in which my brother, my friend, the two police officers, and I all belong—has been so powerful a part of my journey, both for healing and as an activist for social change. I was first introduced to the idea of Beloved Community when I read these words of Dr. Martin Luther King Jr:

> The end is reconciliation; the end is redemption; the end is the creation of the Beloved Community. It is this type of spirit and this type of love that can transform opposers into friends. It is this type of understanding goodwill that will transform the deep gloom of the old age into the exuberant gladness of the new age. It is this love which will bring about miracles in the hearts of men.[1]

As I read various expositions on what Dr. King meant by Beloved Community, I came to an understanding that resonated with me. Beloved Community was, for me, family. Not Norman Rockwell characters gathered around a beautiful table full of food, laughing and smiling at each other with no apparent tension or conflict at all, or the families torn apart by the effects of generations of capitalism and white supremacy ideology, always sniping at each other and jock-eying for status.

Rather, when I think of family as a metaphor for Beloved Community, I think of people, connected by love for each other, whose well-being is intertwined. People who see the full range of each other's human expression, regardless of how we present—angry, sad, happy, scared, in pain. I think of people who know, at a visceral level, that regardless of how much money, resources, or social capital they have, they cannot be happy if anyone in their family is suffering. I think of people who truly understand interdependence, who know that their capacity to thrive is dependent on the actions of others, just as those others are dependent on them. Beloved Community is a world where we see each human as family. Where I'm willing to speak up and tell you when your actions have been too costly for me or those around me and invite you to consider a different action. Where I listen when you call me in, inviting me to notice how my actions impact you and those around you. Where we are willing to engage in the dance of dialogue, moving between empathy and authentic expression, to create a world that works for all.

Dr. King and many others have focused on one aspect of the essential work to create Beloved Community. They speak of the urgency of changing laws, changing the social structures that position some people securely at the table while others scramble outside, hoping to gather enough scraps to survive. Dr. Ibram X. Kendi rightfully decries "uplift suasion," the be-lief that if those from marginalized groups show up in all their strength—smart, accomplished, embodying the characteris-tics of those inside the room—then those in the room would recognize their worth, their humanness, and welcome them in.[2] As Dr. Kendi pointed out, years of research show that what creates a shift in attitudes is not proving to those with power and resources that we're just like them but instead changing laws to mandate entry into the room.[3] Once we're in the room engaging, interacting, and living, attitudes change.

I agree with all of this. Opening the door and creating access is essential, however, it's not enough to create Beloved Community. I think of a family I know. Biologically related, this family had decades-long history of strife. Some folks didn't feel valued by other members. Some members were openly disdainful and excluded other members of the family. For many years some family members were never in the same house at the same time. I was at a dinner that the matriarch of the family had decreed everyone had to attend to honor an elder who had passed. The resulting gathering was as far from Beloved Community as one could imagine. Folks in the room didn't know how to respond when the inevitable misunderstandings arose. They resorted to old patterns—judging, blaming, shaming, attacking. Some folks left early, swearing never to return.

This pattern happens in larger societal configurations when groups come together. I've been in organizations where there's been racial conflict. Folks say they're willing to come to the table, to heal past pain in order to advance their mission. But after the first statement that stimulates pain, however unintentional, people retreat into defensive, closed positions. Despite their stated desire to shift old dynamics, they didn't have the skills to speak up and call in those whose actions were painful for them, and they didn't have the skills to know how to respond differently when harm was named. We often don't know how to set aside the constraining patterns of the world we've been given—one that says some people are bad, hopeless, seek only to take advantage and harm us. We don't know how to step into a world of Beloved Community that lets us see that our healing and liberation is inextricably tied up with the healing and liberation of everyone around us, even those who have caused us harm.

Creating Beloved Community

External change—change to structures and laws that govern how society works—is needed to create Beloved Community. Laws like the Civil Rights Act of 1964—which, among other things, made illegal employment discrimination on the basis of race, color, religion, sex, and national origin—are a crucial step. However, in addition to these external changes, I believe there are internal and interpersonal changes that need to happen. Dr. King identified an important strategy to creating this change: nonviolence. Nonviolence, as the path to creating the changes in social structures that are so urgently needed, sets the stage to create Beloved Community.

What do we mean by "nonviolence"? First, I like to start by saying what nonviolence is *not*. It is not stoic acceptance. It's not sitting back, experiencing harm and inequities, and waiting for people to change. Uplift suasion is a form of that. A Black elder I know speaks about how he was raised. He was told that no matter what a white person did, you accepted it. You didn't protest or raise a fuss—instead, you continued to do what you needed to do to accomplish your goals. In doing so, white folks might feel shame, might come to look past their prejudice and see how you were carrying yourself, acknowledge the amazing things you were doing, and would thus be motivated to change their attitudes toward you and the race. Although there is strength in this perseverance in the face of unbelievable challenge, this degree of acceptance and reliance on hope that the other will recognize and change their behavior is not nonviolence. Nonviolence is also not inaction. It's not avoiding confrontation with those who are taking action that is harmful. So often I hear people complain bitterly to me, stating, "I want to create harmony. I want to be nonviolent" in order to explain why they are not speaking to the person with whom they are unhappy and instead venting to me.

Nonviolence, in the context of antiracist work, is taking powerful action to directly address the causes of harm and inequities. When we take nonviolent action, we can speak up and resist harm while holding a commitment not to do harm to another. When we act from a commitment to nonviolence, we understand that the society we want to create is not possible if all we seek to do is switch who is holding power and who is being harmed. Although that switch may offer relief for those currently being harmed, it does not create a meaningful shift in society. Instead, we're all on the same cosmic scale of privilege and injustice, going back and forth between which group is experiencing inequities and which group is enjoying society's benefits. We can only create a society grounded in Beloved Community when the scale is dismantled altogether so that all can benefit.

Once we have adopted a nonviolent stance, there are a few other frames of consciousness we need to adopt to create Beloved Community. An important one is the shift from an us-versus-them duality or multiplicity to one of shared humanity. Shared humanity does not mean that I don't acknowledge the social and cultural differences that exist. When I look at my siblings, I see each of them as unique individuals with significant variations in how they show up and move through the world. However, even as I recognize these differences, I am always connected to their membership in my family. They are both family members and unique individuals within the family. It is the same for Beloved Community. I can see and honor the various representations of human creativity and expression, the cultural differences in life experience, that manifest in folks from different racial and ethnic backgrounds.

Even as I look at that, I am connected to each group as embodiments of what it means to be human. In fact, I'm aware that the elements that make us human are more salient, and have more consistency in expression, than the elements that sometimes seem to manifest as group differences. Shared humanity does mean searching for the shared elements that connect all of us humans. Many thinkers have identified some of these elements. Dr. Rosenberg, the person who developed the principles and practices of Nonviolent Communication, identified one important element—the needs that motivate the actions of humans around the world.[4]

Regardless of the external differences between humans and between groups of humans, every human needs food, water, air. Every human needs safety, beauty, connection. Every human needs opportunities to contribute to others, acceptance, and knowledge. When I can stay connected to these and the many other facets of our shared humanity, I can recognize myself in another person. I might mourn that they are attending to their human needs by taking actions that are confusing or even abhorrent to me. But even as I mourn and resist those actions, I recognize and value the shared human needs driving the actions. From this place of connection to our shared humanity, I can find a path in which we can work together to find actions that better meet all our needs.

Once we are firmly grounded in our shared humanity—the needs that motivate all our behaviors—we can find ways to step into nonviolent action when our needs are not being met. When I don't recognize another person's shared humanity, it's easy to judge them, to say that they are being selfish, bad, evil. There is a comfort in these kinds of moralistic judgments. If something is painful for me, then I can label whatever is causing my pain as bad. I no longer see the person taking the action or the elements of our shared humanity that are prompting their action. Instead, I can focus just on getting the painful action to stop at any cost. The moralistic judgments we have learned to impose on others serve us, but at a great cost. They support us in noticing when something is not working for us and taking actions to change that behavior. However, moralistic judgments move us away from Beloved Community because they make it all too easy to lump folks into an "other, bad" group that we don't have to care about or engage with.

Of course, we need to have some way to judge when we are being harmed, when something is not working for us. As we work to create Beloved Community, we can move from moralistic judgments toward more needs-based judgments. When something is not working for us, we can go back to those elements that define our shared humanity. We can tune inward and ask, "What is important to me here? What am I longing for that this action is preventing me from having?" And we can ask, "What is the other person longing for that is leading them to take this action?" Instead of seeing a person or action as inherently bad, I can stand fully in my experience and request change while seeing them for their humanness. I'll share an example that illustrates why I would want to put the energy into seeing someone who has harmed me as part of my Beloved Community. I had an experience in college that impacted me for decades. Many years later, I learned that sadly the experience was not unique. I graduated from one of the "elite" high schools in New York City, where my love of English literature and writing was honed. Despite challenges in high school, I always excelled in my English classes. As a sophomore at my local community college, I was excited to take an eighteenth-century literature class. When I learned I could choose any author for the first paper, I chose Jane Austen, the writer whose work I had devoured over and over with my best friend in high school. After proudly submitting what I thought was the best paper of my life, I was shocked when I saw my grade—F—scrawled on the top with no other comments. Naively, I went to the professor, certain it was a mistake, but he told me that he knew I had plagiarized since "Black people don't write like that."

I was devastated. I was convinced something was wrong with me, that there was some way that I had not been "enough" so that he could recognize my talent. I became afraid to write, never voluntarily writing anything, always turning in coursework or reports at the very last possible minute. I spent the next fifteen years judging myself. In order to heal myself and remove the block that so constrained my written expression, I had to free myself from judgments of both myself and that professor. First, I had to stop judging myself as inadequate. Instead of looking at myself and seeing someone who was inherently flawed—not smart enough, not resilient enough, not strong enough—I had to find a way to transform those self-judgments. Once I truly understood that that professor's comment was rooted in white supremacy ideology and not a valid indictment of me, I started hating him, judging him as a racist who had so terribly impacted my life. And I still didn't write—I knew there were others out there like him who would never see me.

I hadn't really transformed my self-judgment. Instead, I shifted my judgments from myself onto that professor. I was living in a world where either I was wrong and bad, or he was a flawed and evil person. Shifting the judgments onto him and beginning to see myself as capable had some positive impact. I began to write a little more, finding "good" folks who were "not racist" to read my writing. And each time I doubted myself, I would remind myself that he was the one who was bad. He was the one who was flawed. That strategy got me writing again, but not in a way that was grounded in the healing and peace that could only come from being part of a Beloved Community. As long as I saw that professor as inherently evil and unredeemable, I was scared. Although I felt empowered to write and begin to share my voice, I was always waiting for the next evil, racist person to show up and tear me down. As long as those people existed, I knew viscerally that I wasn't truly safe.

What truly created a shift for me was learning how to transform, not relocate, my judgments, both of myself and of him. I looked back on all those long years when I silenced my voice, convinced that I was not smart or capable enough to undeniably prove I had value and that I was weaker than other Black folks who had experienced the same kind of racism but wrote unabashedly. Instead of the moralistic judgment that my reaction was completely unhelpful and a sign of weakness, I began searching for those threads of shared humanity I had with other folks, including those who responded differently than I had. I tapped into all the things I was longing for, all that I did not have access to when this situation occurred, that led me to respond in the way that I did. I wanted so desperately to see my self-worth reflected in the eyes of those around me. I wanted to know that I would be treated fairly and be offered helpful feedback that would support my growth. I needed to know I was accompanied by others who shared my understanding that the professor's words were not grounded in any reality I could recognize, and who could support me in navigating the pain of that understanding.

When I think of how much I longed for those things—accurate reflection of my worth, feedback that enables growth, shared reality, and empathy, I feel such deep sorrow for the young adult who was navigating this intensely painful experience alone. In the absence of any support or any hope of getting these needs met, I withdrew from activities like writing to prevent further harm. This made sense. With that realization, I was able to hold my younger self with gentleness and acceptance. But my healing was not done. As long as I conceived of myself and others like me under siege by people I could not even begin to understand, who I could only perceive as evil, I would not feel safe. That world felt unpredictable and completely out of my capacity to impact.

Reclaiming my power meant I also had to take steps to transform my judgments of that professor. I started to get curious. If I were to think of him as a member of my family, one who did something that was devastatingly painful for me, but family nonetheless, I could ask myself, "Why would he do this? What threads of our shared humanity would possibly lead him to act from a place of stereotyped beliefs?" I will never know why he took the actions he did. But I began to imagine. What if he, too, had been a victim of white supremacy beliefs, told over and over again that Black students were inherently not capable? What if that paper was so far above anything he had ever received from a student of any race that he could not imagine a student, much less a student from a race he had been taught to believe was an inferior one, could write it? If he truly believed these things, could he have given me that grade because he was trying to uphold academic integrity?

I can understand how confirmation bias would limit the information this professor took in, causing him to look for information that was congruent with his assumptions about Black people. His inability to see past the stereotypes he held might then contribute to his flawed decision to assign me to what would be, for him, a more predictable role of a Black student who was incapable, a decision that supports both his belief system and the academic system he treasures. I could even imagine that he might see himself as helping me, giving me the F without reporting me to the dean, so that I would learn quickly that plagiarism was easy to catch and avoid more serious consequences down the road. When I started to wonder about those things, I was able to entertain the possibility that tragically the professor was trying to do the best he could from the very limited perspective he had.

This did not mean that I was okay with his actions, however. Imagining these things didn't lessen or invalidate my pain. I continued the work of recognizing and tending to the many ways that, years later, I was still impacted by his action.

I still needed support to work through the self-doubt and procrastination and anger. And I still believed he had a lot of work to do—acknowledge and repair the impact I (and likely many other students) had experienced, grow his awareness of his racist bias and how it fits into a pattern of educational racism, and learn strategies to remove this bias. My considering his perspective was not to drop myself or let him off the hook. Instead, imagining the professor was acting out of care from a place of misinformation gave me some possibilities on how I could approach a dialogue with him. Before I could envision the common threads of Beloved Community that might have motivated him, I had no hope that any dialogue with him would be effective. Once I could connect with his humanity, I saw the possibilities for calling him into a different awareness and understanding of the capabilities of all humans. I could imagine with this new understanding, if his integrity was stimulated, he would mourn the impact of his actions. I could imagine a path where he could become an advocate against the kind of stereotypical beliefs and actions that harmed so many Global Majority students like me.

Contemplating this possibility allowed me to imagine a world where events made sense—tragic and horrible, but conceivable. And it was not a world in which my only choices were to blame myself or blame someone else, where I was always at the mercy of other people's judgment. This allowed me to stand in my own truth when I received racist messages like the one I got from that professor and to entertain hope that as people like him encountered more people like me and were themselves given feedback about the impact of their actions, they could shift. I became more willing to risk sharing my work because I had hope that more people would be able to engage with it fairly, and I knew how to protect myself even if they did not. I slowly began writing, one piece at a time, leading to my ultimate risk in writing—sharing this book.

Transforming judgments was a necessary part of my process, and it's an important practice for those working for Beloved Community. When we transform our judgments, we open the door to dialogue, to invite someone to become aware of the huge cost of their actions and to take steps to change and mitigate that cost. People need to know when and how their actions are impacting others in order to have a hope of changing their behavior. I usually think of this action, of speaking up about harm one is experiencing, as the maintenance work that sustains Beloved Community. A thriving community needs a healthy feedback system. We need to be able to call each other's attention to a part of the community that is out of order and work together to find the steps to fix it. This necessary function is one of the hardest for communities to manage. If we think of community as a complex machine with sentient parts, each part needs to be able to say to the other, "Hey, right now there's a part of you that's rubbing on me this way. It's wearing out this joint and preventing me from moving as fully as I can." And since each part of the machine is committed to the whole Beloved Community's thriving, the part that gets that message would ideally say: "Whoa! Thanks for telling me. Let me adjust to see if this works better for you so we can all be more effective."

Sadly, though, this is not happening. Instead, communities of all sizes and purposes struggle with this essential feedback function. Some parts of the community believe that once a part is no longer working, the best thing to do is to respond harshly. And other parts never learned how to accept feedback openly, without pushing back or crumbling. If the machine could talk, we'd hear the parts utilizing moralistic judgments. Some might say: "Hey, you, over there. You rubbed me in this way. You're bad and you've got to go." Other parts might join in, saying: "Yeah, disconnect it from the rest of us. It's hopelessly bad." And the part that was called out might respond with defensive anger, saying: "You don't know what you're talking about. I'm going to keep doing what I'm doing. You're the one who needs to change." All while pushing harder and causing more harm. Or it might respond with fear—"I am bad. I'm hopeless. I deserve to be an outcast"—and freeze, bringing the whole machine to a halt. This pattern of using moralistic judgments is not helpful. These judgments disrupt the complex machinery of community and cause us to discard community members. If we keep throwing out parts of a machine, eventually we'll have a broken machine, barely achieving its goals, and a collection of discarded parts ready to be picked up and used by someone who might harm us. The current tendency to cast moralistic judgment and blame thus harms our Beloved Community. It fractures us and prevents us from creating a path to true accountability and change, one grounded in acknowledgment and full understanding.

Accountability as a key to Beloved Community is rooted in our awareness of true interdependence. It posits: "I am aware that my thriving is connected to your thriving and yours to mine and that our community cannot thrive if either of us is failing. I acknowledge there are times when I might do things that impact you. I want to know of that impact so that I can take action to address it and return our community to its full strength. In those times when I experience impact from you, I commit to letting you know about it, as often as necessary while continuing to cherish you as a member of my Beloved Community. This allows you to take the actions necessary to address the impact and return our community to full strength."

As we hold to this principle of accountability, we realize the importance of our words and our intentions. I shared my experience with that professor to make evident how moralistic judgments can get in the way of our creating Beloved Community and how needs-based judgments can support necessary change to maintain Beloved Community. It's definitely possible to develop a moralistic attitude toward even that duality: moralistic judgments are "bad" and needs-based judgments are "good." There's only one right way to call someone in and anything else is harsh and bad. Even here, we can take a step back and examine what it means to call someone in or out. We can apply the same framework of looking for the threads of our shared humanity to understand why someone might choose an intense, angry calling out over a gentler, compassionate calling in.

Although we'll explore calling in and calling out in more depth later in this book, it's sufficient now to remind you of a time when you've exploded with anger. Were you feeling hopeless after having repeatedly tried and failed to raise awareness of an issue? Were you responding from a place of deep shock in the face of an unexpected action that stimulated intense pain? Were you deeply afraid, responding from a place of panicky fear that your well-being and possibly even survival were at risk? Responding with harshness in any of these moments is understandable—we've all done it. We might find it easy to hold compassion for someone who shares their pain with a gentle calling in that arises from a place of more emotional resourcedness, practice, or even fear to speak with intensity. But we can also choose to bring equal understanding and compassion to someone who expresses their pain with intensity, even when it might be hard for us to receive the intensity and to choose a different response. As we work to build Beloved Community, we can welcome a fierce authenticity in all its forms, for authentic feedback enables that maintenance work that we need. And we can work to manage our own reactions to the form of the feedback, whether a calling out or calling in, and glean whatever insights the feedback can offer to support our taking actions that align with our values and goals.

As we learn of these elements that are essential to creating and maintaining Beloved Community we may wonder if the effort is worth it. Why would we invest the time and energy, the emotional labor, to see the humanity of those who take actions that result in our harm? Why should we not see this commitment to align with Beloved Community as yet another burden placed on those who are less resourced that makes it easier for those with more resources? We do this because we want to change the habits of dualist thinking, of us versus them, good versus bad, winner or loser, that have defined so many generations of human culture. We can choose to hold only ourselves and members of our communities with the caring, fierce authenticity that can help our communities thrive. But each time we treat those we deem different, bad, irredeemable in ways that ostracize and diminish them, we reinforce that value system in ourselves. The system that says some people are worth saving and some are not.

As that system gets reinforced, in addition to diminishing our effectiveness, it becomes only a matter of time before something we do, or someone else does, causes us to apply that system internally, not just outwardly. We see this as groups fall apart, unable to recover and stay connected to each member's worth when we discover that some folks don't share our preferred strategies, or even more quickly when they do something we don't like. We see it turned inward, as people judge themselves harshly for not meeting some standard, often internalized from white supremacy culture, they have set for themselves, lashing out, checking out, even ending their lives because they don't have the practice of meeting everyone with a compassionate request for change when things are really tough.

Without even knowing it, we have begun to engage in Authentic Dialogue. We are starting to address the element of consciousness here. The more we can practice the elements of Beloved Community with those we struggle to identify with or humanize, the more capacity we build. Chapter 2 takes us into another element of the consciousness of Authentic Dialogue, acknowledging and freeing ourselves from the impact of white supremacy beliefs. For example, knowing about white supremacy culture, if I can find a way to see the humanity of my professor, speak up about the harm I experienced, and let him know what steps would mitigate that harm and prevent future harm, then I will have those skills available to use with any community member whose actions I don't like. I work on creating Beloved Community so that I strengthen the mind-set that lets me have the quality of relationships and trust I seek with those I care about. And as a bonus, when I bring those whom I previously saw as enemies into my Beloved Community, when my fierce authenticity has called them into action and inspired change, then I also have more people who can help me on the long journey to create Beloved Community.

NOTES

1. Martin Luther King Jr., "Facing the Challenge of a New Age." Address delivered at the First Annual Institute on Nonviolence and Social Change, Martin Luther King Jr. Research and Education Institute, Stanford University, May 24, 2021, https://kinginstitute.stanford.edu /king-papers/documents/facing-challenge-new-age-address-delivered -first-annual-institute-nonviolence.

2. Ibram X. Kendi, *Stamped from the Beginning: The Definitive History of Racist Ideas in America* (New York: Bold Type Books, 2017), 124.

3. Kendi, *Stamped from the Beginning,* 508.

4. Marshall B. Rosenberg, *Nonviolent Communication: A Language of Life,* 3rd ed. (Encinitas, CA: PuddleDancer Press, 2015), 178.

2

White Supremacy Ideology as a Block to Dialogue

I came to the United States when I was seven. My voice proudly declared the country of my origin, Trinidad. You could hear my island's rhythms in the musical cadence of my speech. Although I started school in Harlem, where almost all my classmates were Black, most of our teachers were white. I was a strong student, in part because my US school insisted on placing me in second grade because I was small rather than place me in the fourth grade classroom that was analogous to the fourth standard classroom I had been in at home. Despite excelling at schoolwork, adults in my school decided that something was wrong with me. My accent was deemed problematic, so I was sent to speech therapy where I learned to speak "correctly." It wasn't until much later that I realized I learned to speak with the same accent the white teachers and speech therapist used. What made a group of adults decide that my Trini accent was inferior, problematic, bad? And once they decided that, why was I taught to speak not like the other students in my community, with Black American accents and dialects, but like the white teachers and professionals in the school? What made one accent better and "proper" while another one was deemed lesser that would hold me back from success?

This pervasive experience of white supremacy ideology—the belief that things associated with whiteness were good and those associated with Blackness were inferior—continued as the years unfolded. In seventh grade I was teased by white students who called me "Snuffleupagus" after the long-nosed Sesame Street character because my nose and lips were "too big." In ninth grade classmates labeled my athletic, developing body "fat" because it did not look like the willowy, thigh-gapped body standard they were taught to revere. In tenth grade I smiled outwardly, while wincing internally, each time my white boyfriend called me "treasure troll" whenever I wore my hair unconfined. In high school I resisted attempts to make me drop out of the neuropsychopharmacology course that my classmates were taking because someone thought I would struggle with it, despite having grades similar to others enrolled with no conflict. In graduate school a classmate dismissed me when I said I was worried about getting a job after graduate school by saying, "You don't have to worry. You'll get a job because of affirmative action." Years later, after bonding with my husband's white family over our excitement about President Obama's candidacy, I fell silent when one person gushed, "He's so handsome, for a Black man."

And on and on. All these incidents have an underlying message. Black is bad, lesser than, not as beautiful, capable, accomplished. White is good, better than, brilliant, wonderful, exciting—the standard against which others must be measured. How did these beliefs become so pervasive in US society that they touch so many areas—our schools, homes, health care systems, relationships, religious institutions, careers? Before we explore how to talk about these experiences, to stop them from affecting future generations the way I was impacted, we need to understand how this belief in white supremacy became part of the culture of the United States and much of the world.

Isabel Wilkerson frames race relations in the United States as an "American caste system, an artificial hierarchy in which most everything that you could and could not do was based upon what you looked like."[1] She notes that the original aim of the caste system in the United States was to benefit the colonists searching for a predictable, controllable source of labor. As Wilkerson describes, since English and Irish enslaved and indentured folks had phenotypes that looked similar to those who were enslaving them, they often ran away and merged invisibly into the larger population. They were thus unpredictable labor sources. The enslaved Africans, however, had a distinguishing phenotype—skin color—that was different from those enslaving them. By choosing color as a defining characteristic of who could be enslaved for life and who might be indentured, but could earn freedom from servitude, the colonists established a source of labor that could not easily escape because they could be easily identified. Therefore, a source of folks that the colonists could continue to enslave simply by virtue of their skin color ensured an always flowing labor pipeline. For most people a belief in white supremacy was not a conscious, premeditated strategy. Instead, it was—and is—an unquestioned, accepted framing of the world that, because of its social acceptance, met needs for cognitive, emotional, and ultimately physical comfort for those who were—and are—white.

The institution of slavery was not new to the world. Across millennia, war and enslavement were some of the horrific strategies used to gain control of and develop resources. One thing that differentiated slavery in the colonies from the enslavement of previous times was that most earlier forms of slavery represented who had power and who did not. In China's Han dynasty, for example, those who were enslaved did not differ in ethnicity from those who enslaved them. Criminals were punished by having their relatives sold into slavery; poor people sometimes sold their children into slavery. In Roman times, for instance, poor people also might sell their children into slavery; other people who were captured by pirates or during war were enslaved. While some ancient civilizations such as the Greeks and the Moors used group differences such as location, ethnic affiliation, skin color, and religion to justify enslaving people, the construction and use of racist ideas to justify slavery emerged in the 1400s, fueled by the burgeoning Atlantic slave trade, and was brought to the Americas.[2]

Of course, this idea that an external characteristic like skin color was justification for enslaving people made no sense. Ibram X. Kendi argues that a belief system had to be created to justify this—thus the myth of white superiority and Black inferiority was born. Skin color became the ideal justification for slavery because skin color was arguably one signifier of a host of differences. If folks with dark skin are different—physically stronger, capable of thriving in harsh conditions, less sensitive to pain, ineducable, without emotions—then it's clear they are not like white people and thus not truly human. And if they are not human, then like any other animal they can be bought and sold. As Kendi lays out so beautifully, the colonists and Europeans worked hard to frame Black people as inferior—morally, spiritually, intellectually, and physically. If one could be brought to believe in a superior white human race and an inferior Black subhuman race, then there would be no moral impediment to the justification of slavery. The need to justify the institution of slavery created the myth of white supremacy. The country's ongoing reliance on the institution for its growth kept fueling that myth.[3]

If we no longer have the institution of slavery, why does the myth of white supremacy still persist and show up in so many spheres of modern life? One of the core principles of Nonviolent Communication is that every action humans take is to meet a need. If we think about a belief in white supremacy as an action, there are several goals that are met by this belief. A person might look around and see that their life does not mirror the American dream. Instead of the house, two cars in the garage, and a family, they are barely making ends meet, struggling sometimes even at a basic survival level. If that person looks around and compares themselves to others—those around them and those fictional successful folks on television, then a belief in white supremacy reassures them that no matter how bad their life seems in comparison, it's better than a Black person's life. For some white folks who have not found their path to success, a belief in white supremacy is a path to acceptance, hope, and positive self-regard. It helps to define their sense of self and bolsters a shared identity that attends to the natural desire for acceptance and belonging we all have.[4]

Just like the enslavers during this country's colonial era and beyond, there are others today who profess to believe in white supremacy because doing so helps them to gain and hold onto power. If they continue the narrative that Black and Brown folks are subhuman and thus not eligible for basic human rights, then it makes it possible to continue to engage in practices that enrich themselves at horrific costs to members of those groups. When these folks in power consider how to ensure that their legislation and policies continue to prop up their practices, they often further the narrative of the dangerous Black savage that must be guarded against. This mobilizes many people to support those policies and to elect those who would be aligned with their goals, even when the legislation and policies actually harm the well-being of those mobilized in support of them. We saw this, for example, when 50 percent of white Americans voiced opposition to the federal Affordable Care Act and Medicaid expansion, an opposition that was more prevalent in conservative states with greater degrees of racial resentment.[5]

The 2016 presidential election of Donald Trump is a classic example of the intersection of these patterns. Given the stories we have heard of Trump's childhood and young adulthood, in which he strove unsuccessfully to gain his father's love, one path toward his father's acceptance might have been to buy into the myth of white supremacy that Trump saw his father embody. And as Trump aligned himself with these beliefs, he used them to bolster his appeal to certain people and influence business deals. German Lopez reports that Trump gained regional and national publicity through his actions grounded in white supremacist ideals. These include taking out an ad in newspapers seeking the death penalty in the Central Park Five case for the Black and Latino teens who were later proved to be innocent of any crime; and promoting the racist accusations that Barack Obama was not born in the

United States.[6] These types of actions kept Trump popular with a certain crowd and eventually led to millions of people cheering him on in admiration, ultimately elevating Trump to the presidency. There was a symbiotic relationship there. Trump and his followers were able to establish a powerful sense of community and belonging, and both Trump and his followers gained access or seeming proximity to power that they would not have been able to gain without mobilizing others against Black and Brown people.

As long as people believe in white supremacy ideology and experience benefits (even unknowingly) from these beliefs and practices, we will struggle to stamp out white supremacy culture. White supremacy ideas are woven into the very fabric of the United States, and indeed these beliefs are woven into the fabric of much of the rest of the world as well. Even those of us who are actively trying to lift up a more accurate understanding of the world are impacted by white supremacy ideas in the institutions and social structures we are part of, in the ways some of us are privileged and others burdened as we navigate those structures, and in the challenges to our interpersonal connections with people we encounter as we move through our days. In order to eradicate white supremacy ideology, we must acknowledge and actively confront the ways the system of beliefs manifests personally, interpersonally, and structurally.

As I travel the world to share this work, I repeatedly encounter the belief that talking about racism is what perpetuates racism and that challenging the notion of race, or a race-blind approach, is what will eliminate it. There are two main stances that people, both white and Global Majority, hold. In the first, people claim that we are living in a postracial society, pointing to achievements such as Barack Obama's presidency and the appointments of Sonia Sotomayor and Ketanji Brown Jackson to the US Supreme Court. This idea of a postracial society depends on the belief that structural racism no longer exists. For some, this implies that the only thing preventing Global Majority folks from doing as well as white folks on a wide variety of metrics (e.g., educational, health, occupational, financial) is lack of effort on their part. In the second stance, others acknowledge that while racism may still exist, it is primarily a reflection of people's attitudes and beliefs, not of structures and systems. These people argue that the end of racism will result through insisting on color blindness—refusing to ask about or look at race despite disparities. Proponents of that strategy have passed laws that restrict collecting or using information about race, with diverse impacts such as making it illegal to collect information on race when hiring people, to put on a workshop just for Black or Brown people, or to look at race when making admissions or scholarship decisions. France is an example of this strategy, even going so far as to remove the word "race" from its constitution.[7]

Both stances on a race-blind approach are flawed. First, let's examine the claim that we live in a postracial society. The continued rise in individual and group hate crimes and murders since President Obama's inauguration provides simple proof. The Equal Justice Initiative has analyzed FBI statistics that show the highest number of reported hate crimes since 2008 took place in 2021, with hate crimes because of race increasing between 2019 and 2021 more than any other category of hate crime.[8] Similarly, the idea that Global Majority folks would be successful if they only worked harder has been debunked. The Brookings Institute summarized in 1998 several studies that showed the key factor impacting the achievement of Black and Brown students was the amount of money spent in their school districts, which influences class size, teacher qualification, and the quality of the curriculum. When all else holds equal, Global Majority students who are given access to more challenging work by prepared teachers in smaller classes do as well as their white counterparts.[9]

These disparities are compounded by the subtle effects of a belief in white supremacy. The Brookings Institute analyzed data from the Implicit Association Test, Stanford Data Archive, and Civil Rights Data Collection to look at the relationship between implicit bias, student achievement, and student discipline. Brookings found that even after controlling for confounding factors like poverty, Black students did more poorly on tests and received higher rates of suspension in counties where teachers demonstrated more pro-white / anti-Black implicit bias.[10] Taken together, this research helps to explain the underachievement of so many Global Majority students.

My own educational experience demonstrates the ways these factors impact the achievement of students throughout their educational careers. My elementary school in Harlem in New York City was poorly funded and could not meet the needs of most of the students in the school. I was successful not just on my own merits, but because I was the only child in my elementary school selected to participate in an academic enrichment program that provided the high-quality instruction and enriched curriculum my specific school could not. And although I worked as hard as my peers once I tested into the city's elite schools, I was implicitly and explicitly directed to "easier" classes. It would be simple in the current meritoc-racy to believe that I earned my PhD because I was a hard worker. But I know otherwise. I earned it because I was given opportunities that very few of my peers received. I was fortu-nate to find teachers and professors who actively confronted bias and nurtured my journey.

The other concern—that talking about or tracking race is what causes racism—is also incorrect. It may be true that the naming of a thing helps to give it life. In this case, however, the belief in white supremacy already exists. Its existence has led to (and continues to lead to) myriad abuses of Global Majority people. When we name the huge costs and dispari-ties that result from practices embedded in white supremacy beliefs, we bring to life an awareness of the practices, not the practices themselves. With greater awareness, we can seek to eradicate them. Communities that don't collect or track data on race in education, housing, employment, and more might find it easy to say that they don't have problems with race. However, with the statistics gathered by Equal Justice Initia-tive and other organizations, it's clear that these problems do exist, but there is no way to talk about them without it being dismissed as anecdotal.

Connection Blocks to Combating
White Supremacy Beliefs and Practices

One of the goals of the white supremacy narrative—the idea that things associated with whiteness are superior to those associated with any other ethnic group—is to prevent peo-ple from connecting across differences. It is much easier to keep one group subjugated, and another group willing to subjugate, if the two groups are prevented from connecting in any meaningful way. Actual physical divides are an obvious way of supporting white supremacy beliefs through disconnection. When communities are segregated from each other, it can be hard to even meet folks from a different group than one's own. In my elementary school in Harlem, from second through sixth grade, the only white people I saw were the teachers. In middle and high school I gained access to schools with stronger academic programs, but that came at a cost: Black students were fewer than 6 percent of the class in these schools.

This kind of segregation is still evident in many areas across the United States. In 2019 only 7 of the 895 students admitted to the high school I attended were Black.[11] Historical redlining has an enduring impact evidenced by ongoing physical segregation and the defunding of Global Majority neighborhoods. Education is defunded in some communities causing wealthier, and often whiter, families to leave. Physical segregation is itself a large part of the problem. We can't have the dialogues and exchanges that will dismantle white supremacy culture if we're not even in the room together. This is, in part, why legal and structural change must happen. We all need to be at the table for things to change. Even when we're sitting at the same table, however, there are several beliefs and ways of interacting that effectively block the kinds of connections that can challenge the narrative of white supremacy.

Connection Block 1: Dualistic Thinking

Dualistic thinking is the either/or framing that we use to understand and justify so much of what happens in the world.

People are either good or bad. You're either Black or white. You're either liberal or conservative. As we keep working in these rigid categories, we assign value to them. Depending on our perspective, maybe a person is liberal = good versus conservative = bad—maybe it's the other way around for you. Either you share our values or you're the evil, brainwashed, uneducated other. When we insist on these either/or differences, we lose the capacity to meet people at a human level. There's no room in the simplified, dualistic world for the conservative supporter of abortion rights or the liberal gun owner.

And in conversations about race, this dualistic thinking is especially dangerous. It leads us to reject or cancel the person who unconsciously does something that lands as a microaggression. It makes us reject the person who isn't behaving in ways that conform to our beliefs about how someone from their group should behave. It leads us to be afraid of speaking up and acknowledging when we don't know something, concerned that we will be labeled bad or unsalvageable. As long as we keep believing that there is a right way or a wrong way to be, and that only those who embrace the right path are worth connecting with, we make it near impossible to reach out to those whom we perceive are on a different path than we are. This is especially unfortunate since this way of thinking leads us to quickly assign so many to that outgroup.

Connection Block 2: The Belief in Scarcity

Another way white supremacy beliefs keep us divided is by furthering the myth that there is not enough to go around. This myth is a natural outgrowth from dualistic thinking. As we interact with systems that are set up to ensure that some people don't have access to what they need to thrive, the prevalent belief in scarcity that is foundational to our societies becomes a way to justify those systems. If we were aligned with life's natural abundance, however, we might challenge those systems. If there is not enough food, water, energy, quality housing, or education—of course it makes sense that scarce resources can't be divided. As long as we believe that there is not enough, we buy into the struggle. Either I get what I need and you don't, or you get what you need and I don't.

At the high school I attended, for example, where admission is based on the results of a single high-stakes test, some parents and educators advocate for changing that system, while others are vehemently opposed. The underlying reason for this opposition is this belief in scarcity: there are only so many spots available at these elite schools, so any change that would make it easier for the sorely underrepresented Black, Latine, and Indigenous students to enter means taking spots away from Asian and white students. If we believe that access to quality education is a scarce resource, we focus on ensuring that our child, or the members of our own community, have access to that resource, instead of questioning the underlying assumption that quality education should be a scarce resource at all. With all the resources available in our world, there's absolutely no logical reason why we can't do a much better job of creating a system that can support the learning needs of all of our children.

This belief in scarcity, with each group doing its best to protect limited access, perpetuates the pattern that underlies the narrative of white supremacy in the first place. This scarcity myth establishes a system where we are told to believe that some people will gain access to resources and others won't, and we justify lack of access by claiming it's caused by inherent flaws in those who don't have access. Going back to the education system, some folks argue that white and Asian students pass the test because they work hard, while the Black and Latine students don't pass because they don't put in the effort. Instead, people should be asking, "How can we make an education system that really supports all students?" We don't question a system that makes amazing educational resources available to some groups but not others. Rather, we accept that the system works, and that the outcome is confirmation of who deserves their place and who does not.

Connection Block 3: Prioritizing Process over Content

One way to unintentionally, and at times intentionally, interrupt conversations about racism and other inequities is through an insistence on a certain process or form for these conversations. Not surprisingly, the form that is often chosen is one that favors ways of being that are typical of those with more structural power and prioritizes processes that ensure the comfort of those with power. I have been brought into organizations by folks who are concerned about complaints of racial inequities lodged by a person from the Global Majority. Invariably, when those who are bringing me in describe the concerns, they may acknowledge the legitimacy of the issues being raised but often add the part that led them to bring me in. "We're grateful Person X brought this to our attention, but he's going about it all wrong. Everyone feels scared now." Or "She's so angry. She's not following the right procedures, so it keeps interrupting our meetings and our work." When I ask what the person is doing, I might be told, "Well, they bring it up again and again in the staff meetings." Or "They got really upset and yelled once." Or "They repeatedly point out whenever they think someone is doing something racist."

As I hear this, I imagine the person they are describing as someone who is desperately trying to raise awareness that might lead to change; someone who is yearning to be met with some response that acknowledges their experiences and the severe impact they have felt. And instead, this person is consistently met with messages that do the opposite. "Yes, this is important, but you shouldn't raise your voice in staff meetings. Everyone has a right to a safe workplace." Can you imagine how you might feel if that's the response you get when you raise your voice because you have been repeatedly harmed? The underlying message the person from the Global Majority might perceive is "It's okay if you or people like you experience harm while we figure out some ways to look at this problem that keep everyone else emotionally safe. Everyone *but* you deserves a safe workplace." The rapid, disapproving response to the ways messages are delivered, combined with glacial attention to the content of those messages, often reinforces the implicit message of whose well-being is valued and who needs and receives support. Similar impacts occur when meetings are called to address these issues.

Some of these meetings are highly structured, with rigid rules to follow of who speaks when. Global Majority folks experience being interrupted, cut off, told they are speaking out of turn or off-topic at the same time white folks are permitted to go off-topic, or take longer than their allotted time without repercussion. In public formal meetings, for example, insistence on following a form not everyone knows and can anticipate means that folks with structural power get up or otherwise signal they want to speak and get queued up in order to do so while folks without knowledge of the system find themselves at the back of the queue, subject to not being heard because time has run out. This essentially uses the process to reinforce whose voice is prioritized, at the expense of content. When we insist on rules, or don't ensure that everyone has the same information, we privilege some folks (typically those with more structural power) over others (those with less structural power, often Global Majority folks).

Connection Block 4: Conflating the Systemic and the Individual

In March 2022, Florida's legislature passed the Stop W.O.K.E. Act, banning educational or employment programs that would lead someone to feel "discomfort, guilt, anguish, or any other form of psychological distress on account of his or her race, color, sex, or national origin."[12] This legislation is a prime example of an erroneous conflation of the systemic and the individual. This occurs when we attack the individual for the existence of systemic problems. Racism and white supremacy beliefs have been the source of unimaginable suffering for countless people around the world. A compassionate person who truly sees that depth of suffering would, and arguably should, feel something! The conditions we feel distressed about exist whether or not we are aware of them. It is only through raising awareness that people not directly impacted by these conditions can be moved to take action in solidarity. Florida's legislative stance asserts that the individual or action raising awareness of systemic inequities is as bad as the inequities themselves. It shifts the "blame" for our feelings of discomfort from the existence of these conditions to the person who calls our awareness to the conditions. Instead of saying, "I feel distressed that these inequities exist in the world," people instead say, "I feel distressed that you made me think about these conditions."

A similar conflation of the systemic and the individual occurs when people who are asked to look at the ways they benefit from systemic inequities interpret that to mean that they are being accused of being racist. We live in a society that affords some people benefits based on their group membership. When attempts are made to show how white folks have benefited systemically at the expense of other groups, some people say, "Are you saying I'm racist?" or "That was before my time. I didn't benefit from it." There is a fear that acknowledging that one has benefited from the racial disparities that exist in modern life is tantamount to acknowledging that one is racist. A person can benefit from policies that they had no hand in creating (and might even be working against), independent of whether or not they themselves are currently engaged in racist actions.

Connection Block 5: The Tyranny of Intensity

I facilitated a workshop for Black and white women who wanted to figure out how to work together to advance antiracist practices in their community. I met with the Black women first. Many were worried about meeting with the white women since they did not trust that, despite the stated intention of the gathering, either group of women would be able to transcend the racial rules that had governed their lives. When the groups finally came together, a Black elder said that she wanted to see the white women interact with her and the other Black women as people, not tokenized Black folks who could help the white women achieve their agenda without any interactions outside that setting.

This elder Black woman was met with confusion and resistance. "We see you. We want to know about your history, about your experiences." The white women asked the Black women to talk about their experiences of racism and to trust that they would be heard. When one of the Black women expressed angrily that the white women's focus on only talking about race was getting in the way of being known for all of what she brings to the community, the white woman she was speaking to burst into tears. And, as has happened many times, the white woman's tears of distress pulled several people into caring for her, while the Black woman's distress was ignored. This is an all-too-common example of the tyranny of intensity. We live in a culture that has long valued white people's needs, physical and emotional, over those of other folks. Dr. Myisha Cherry talks about the unspoken racial rules emerging from the institution of slavery that continue to influence modern society. Dr. Cherry describes rules that state who has value (white folks) and who does not (Black folks); who is allowed to be angry (white folks) and who cannot be angry (Black folks).[13] One of the Black elders articulated a similar rule in the workshop that day: "We're not allowed to make white women upset." She meant that no matter what the white women said or did, the Black women were supposed to accept it. In such a climate, this means that conversation can only occur as long as white folks are comfortable.

Many Global Majority people, not just Black folks, find themselves impacted by or even unconsciously following these rules. If a Global Majority person wants to talk about race, they can do so up to the point that the white person gets upset. And if the white person is upset, the conversation shifts from addressing the content the Global Majority person wanted to address to mitigating the white person's distress— thus becoming another manifestation of the connection block that prioritizes process over content. One can imagine that true conversation about difficult topics cannot take place if one group's comfort is prioritized over any meaningful content. If my rage as a Black person faced with seeing yet another Black person killed results in a white person's discomfort, how can I ever speak about that rage and despair and longing for Black lives to be valued? We cannot have meaningful conversations about race if we do not have the capacity to hold our own and others' intensity. Instead of letting a desire to avoid intensity determine when dialogue must end, it is imperative for us to learn how to welcome intensity and use it to access deeper connection and truth-telling.

As this chapter explored, white supremacy beliefs and practices are deeply embedded into our culture and systems. Even as some of the more overt manifestations of these practices have been challenged and dismantled (e.g., the institution of chattel slavery and laws that expressly privilege white people over Global Majority folks), systems and individual behaviors shaped by these beliefs are endemic. As James Baldwin wrote: "Not everything that is faced can be changed. But nothing can be changed until it is faced."[14] The Authentic Dialogue framework asks us to hold an intention to work toward our collective liberation by exploring the pervasiveness of white supremacy culture and beliefs in our lives and our interactions, and to acknowledge and attempt to address them if we determine they are present.

NOTES

1. Isabel Wilkerson, *Caste: The Origins of Our Discontents* (New York: Random House, 2020), 26.

2. Ibram X. Kendi, *Stamped from the Beginning: The Definitive History of Racist Ideas in America* (New York: Bold Type Books, 2017), 22–46.

3. Kendi, *Stamped from the Beginning*, 22–57.

4. Wes Enzinna, "Inside the Radical, Uncomfortable Movement to Reform White Supremacists," *Mother Jones*, July 11, 2018, https://www.motherjones.com/politics/2018/07/reform-white-supremacists-shane-johnson-life-after-hate/.

5. Kevin Fiscella, "Why Do So Many White Americans Oppose the Affordable Care Act?" *American Journal of Medicine* 129, no. 5 (May 1, 2016), https://doi.org/10.1016/j.amjmed.2015.08.041.

6. German Lopez, "Donald Trump's Long History of Racism, from the 1970s to 2020," *Vox*, updated August 13, 2020, https://www.vox.com/2016/7/25/12270880/donald-trump-racist-racism-history.

7. Rokhaya Diallo, "Opinion | France's Dangerous Move to Remove 'Race' from Its Constitution," *Washington Post*, October 28, 2021, https://www.washingtonpost.com/news/global-opinions/wp/2018/07/13/frances-dangerous-move-to-remove-race-from-its-constitution/.

8. Aaryn Urell, "FBI Reports Hate Crimes at Highest Level in 12 Years," Equal Justice Initiative, June 3, 2022, https://eji.org/news/fbi-reports-hate-crimes-at-highest-level-in-12-years/.

9. Linda Darling-Hammond, "Unequal Opportunity: Race and Education," Brookings, July 28, 2016, https://www.brookings.edu/articles/unequal-opportunity-race-and-education/.

10. Tasminda K. Dhaliwal, Mark J. Chin, Virginia S. Lovison, and David M. Quinn, "Educator Bias Is Associated with Racial Disparities in Student Achievement and Discipline," Brookings, March 9, 2022, https://www.brookings.edu/blog/brown-center-chalkboard/2020/07/20/educator-bias-is-associated-with-racial-disparities-in-student-achievement-and-discipline/.

11. Valerie Strauss, "7 Out of 895—the Number of Black Students Admitted to NYC's Most Selective High School. And There Are More Startling Stats," *Washington Post*, March 21, 2019, https://www.washingtonpost.com/education/2019/03/21/out-number-black-students-admitted-nycs-most-selective-high-school-there-are-more-startling-stats/.

12. Tim Craig, "Florida Legislature Passes Bill That Limits How Schools and Workplaces Teach about Race and Identity," *Washington*

Post, March 11, 2022, https://www.washingtonpost.com/nation/2022/03
/10/florida-legislature-passes-anti-woke-bill/. Manny Diaz, "Florida
Senate—2022 SB 148," Calendar for 11/27/2022—The Florida Senate,
https://www.flsenate.gov/Session/Bill/2022/148/BillText/Filed/HTML
(accessed November 27, 2022), lines 71–72.

13. Myisha V. Cherry, "Breaking Racial Rules through Rage," Reynolds Lecture, Learning On Demand, Elon University, April 2019, https://
blogs.elon.edu/ondemand/breaking-racial-rules-through-rage-myisha
-cherry/ (accessed November 27, 2022).

14. James Baldwin, "As Much Truth as One Can Bear," *New York
Times Book Review,* January 14, 1962, p. 38, https://nyti.ms/3imS51K.

3

Choosing Beloved Community

When my youngest was six months old, our family moved from Raleigh, North Carolina, to a small Silicon Valley town. I looked up the population statistics for that county and wondered if my family would find a welcome in a place whose population was 3 percent African American. In that town, as it turned out, we experienced so many microaggressions, negative behaviors, and offensive comments tied to our race (see Chapter 8 for more on microaggressions). I managed to ignore or not respond to most of them, even when I was angry or hurt inside. There were a few times when I did not stay silent, however.

The kids usually attended various day camps in the summer. One hectic morning I dropped them off at a camp in a wealthier part of town. After whirlwind mornings getting three kids dressed and fed, finding lost items, and navigating rush hour traffic, the quiet half hour following drop-off was my cherished time. I often sat in my car with a coffee, listening to whatever discussion was happening on NPR. This particular morning, I parked outside a neighborhood coffee shop, waiting for a break in the engrossing story so I could run in to pick up my coffee. As I listened, I saw an elderly woman inside the café walking toward the door, each hand full. I jumped out of the car to open the door. As she exited the coffee shop, she looked down and saw a banana peel on the ground nearby. Instead of thanking me for opening the door, she glared at me and said, "You people always make such messes! Why can't you put your garbage in the garbage can?"

Stunned and angry, I had a split second to decide. How should I respond? Should I say anything to her? That time, at that moment, I responded angrily. "This is not my garbage. Who do you mean when you say 'you people'? Do you think because I'm Black, I had to be eating a banana, like a monkey? Why would you even assume it's my garbage?" As you might imagine, she didn't respond to my questions, instead walking off with a huff. And I was okay with that. In hindsight, I realized I had not really wanted to engage with her. I spoke up in that moment driven by my desire to be seen, to acknowledge—even if just to myself—that racist assumptions were at play here, in protest against the many moments of violence I encountered throughout my days in that community. My expression accomplished all of that for me, but a core need remained unmet.

Both my silence and my angry response in the face of microaggressions had one thing in common. Neither were effective in creating the world I so desperately longed for—one in which my children, all children, could grow up knowing they were fully accepted and that their full humanity and gifts would be seen and nurtured. Instead, my responses demonstrated the tension between positive peace and negative peace Dr. King discussed in 1956.[1] The woman's angry expression and my frustrated retort in response, both making visible the racial tension in our interaction, would not be judged as peaceful by most folks. She and I likely each left with a sense that we were not seen for who we are, with a story that the other had acted violently. I know I did not view this woman as a valued member of my community, and I doubt she saw me in that way.

Some people would tell me I could have stayed silent, walked away, given her the benefit of the doubt. That, however, would be settling for negative peace—the seeming absence of tension and conflict and a sense of personal safety. I still would have been impacted by the stereotypes I perceived in her assumptions, but by staying silent and turning away, I could maintain the fiction for both of us that there was no tension or violence happening. This kind of peace does not create change. Dr. King spoke to this when he said: "I come not to bring this peace of escapism, this peace that fails to confront the real issues of life, the peace that makes for stagnant complacency.... Peace is not merely the absence of some negative force—war, tension, confusion, but it is the presence of some positive force—justice, goodwill, the power of the kingdom of God."[2]

I don't want to settle for negative peace—silence and acceptance in the face of harm and suffering. Instead, in order to build Beloved Community, we must work to create a peace that is built on justice, on care, on truly working to attend to the needs of all beings. The positive peace on which Beloved Community is built requires not our silence but our action. It depends on us to speak up, to interrupt, to name and address harm when we encounter it. And it requires us to become vocal, to welcome the inevitable tension, discomfort, and even pain. It demands of us that we work to change structures and engage in the necessary dialogue for as long as it takes to create a system built on equity and justice for all that doesn't continue to result in some folks experiencing violence in any of its forms.

Thinking about the ideas of positive and negative peace, ending violence in all its forms, and furthering justice to create Beloved Community, it is necessary to understand what we mean by "violence." So often I'm met with confusion—and at times an outright denial—when I frame certain actions or behaviors as violent. Dr. Marshall Rosenberg suggests that violence is "a tragic expression of our own needs and values."[3] In his words we find some key elements to an understanding of violence that can advance positive peace in ways that align with our vision of Beloved Community. First, we realize that people who commit violent actions are doing so in an attempt to meet those universal needs we all have. Violence occurs when someone takes action they believe will attend to their needs in ways that result in unwanted unmet needs for themselves or others. This often happens when the person taking that action is unable to conceive of a different strategy to get their needs met that would not have a cost to others.

Using this definition, violence can range from large to minuscule in its impact, and can be directed toward oneself, others, groups, communities, and even entire countries. This framing of violence encompasses many things that we already unquestionably accept as violence. One nation's war against another is an attempt by some folks in that nation to meet their needs (e.g., to gain access to resources that can help their citizens thrive, to gain freedom to express certain values, and so on) at the expense of both those in their country and the country they fight against. At minimum, war is a tragically costly strategy to meet needs as soldiers and residents on both sides die or are injured (unmet needs for health, well-being, life!) in order for some residents in one country to possibly better meet their needs. War results in the destruction of nonhuman life and damages the necessary land and infrastructure that provides so many with food, clean water, goods, energy. It's clear that even when one side declares victory in a war, it comes at tragic cost. As a result of war, so many folks on both the "losing" and "winning" sides will not have the capacity to meet their basic needs. Similarly, gross acts of violence—murder, rape, enslavement, deforestation, and so on—are all attempts, whether direct or indirect, conscious or unconscious, to meet needs that result in disastrous impact.

Other forms of violence might be less easily recognized but still fit the pattern of someone's needs being met at the cost of other needs going unmet. A subtle example might be the violence we do to ourselves. As a teenager, navigating schools where I did not seem to belong to any community and where so many teachers did not seem to recognize my capacities, I came home most days feeling sad and lonely. I didn't know how to make sense of the unending microaggressions I received—comments about my skin color, hair, lips, size of my nose, motivation, and intelligence; not being called on by teachers, no matter how often I raised my hand; the numerous events my peers attended that I was not invited to; my invitations being turned down because my neighborhood was deemed "unsafe." My teenage self, yearning to make sense of the world, decided that there must be something wrong with me. I wasn't smart enough, thin and pretty enough, kind and accommodating enough, rich enough, from a good enough neighborhood, and so on. *I wasn't enough.*

This belief in my inadequacy was my young self's attempt to make sense of a world that seemed to be rejecting me. If

I were the problem, it would be possible for me to "fix" myself in order to fit in. If I could judge myself harshly enough, I would be motivated to work harder, try harder, be more accommodating, and so forth. I needed hope and a sense of a shared understanding of how the world worked. Putting myself down and prioritizing others' needs over mine gave me a sense of congruence with how others seemed to see me and offered me hope that I could adapt and earn my way into being valued and loved.

I have a lot of compassion for my teen self and for the many people struggling to find belonging and acceptance today. Although I felt some sense of hope that things might improve through focusing on what I then viewed as my flaws, this is an example of heartbreaking self-violence—a result of so many deeply unmet needs. I was not able to meet my own needs for self-acceptance, for mattering, for celebration of who I was. I stopped seeing my own competence. Everything I did was judged against a rubric of "Did it make people like me more?" If the answer was no, it resulted in an affirmation of my incompetence and failure. I sacrificed core needs, like sleep and choice, to do whatever was asked of me to prove that I had value. The harm to my sense of self and my body was incalculable and, decades later, I still struggle to repair that harm.

Violence is taking action to meet some needs that results in unmet needs for others that they did not choose to experience. We go through life often consenting to have some of our needs unmet in order to attend to different needs for ourselves and others. As a mom, for example, my young children cried when they needed my attention in the middle of the night. I willingly gave up sleep to care for them and did not experience their cries as an act of violence. At a different time, I was woken up repeatedly to meet my partner's needs for support during one of our intense periods of conflict, no matter how often I stated I needed to sleep in order to work and care for the kids the next day. I experienced my partner's attempts to get support at the expense of my sleep, in the face of my clear no, as violence. Both my partner and my children needed support that resulted in my unmet needs for sleep, but I only experienced as violence the attempts that ignored my consent.

Of course, this can be multilayered. A parent who has been forced out of work because of their efforts to start a union might go hungry in order to feed their child. They may willingly endure their hunger as their child eats the scarce food as a willingly borne cost to meet their needs for love and care for their child's well-being. And, they may also experience their hunger as violence when they connect it to the employer's attempts to meet the employer's needs for choice and predictability in how the business is run by controlling who works there and has access to jobs that can provide resources for food.

Violence can occur at many levels and in many ways (Figure 2). A colleague at the annual Nonviolent Leadership for Social Justice retreat, Edmundo Norte, uses a model that combines a traditional Indigenous description of aspects of humans often represented on the Medicine Wheel (mental, emotional, spiritual, and physical) with areas of influence (intrapersonal, interpersonal, and institutional) to talk about the places we can direct our attention as we work to attend to impact and well-being.[4] I've used Norte's model to make clearer the many forms of violence that we might experience or commit. When we talk about violence, it can be easy to acknowledge violence that happens in one aspect of life but not others. We often clearly identify violence occurring on the physical aspect but might struggle to recognize or admit to violence taking place on the spiritual or cultural aspect. Similarly, we might be eager to call out violence that happens on a systemic/organizational level but be less able to see violence occurring at the intrapersonal level.

I worked with an organization that brought me in to help them address instances of anti-Blackness that had been occurring, acts the organization clearly identified as violence. Everyone agreed that emotional violence was happening at the structural level. Black people who spoke with intensity about their experiences were reprimanded and censured for "unprofessional behavior." Other types of violence were occurring, in part as a response to the structural violence, but were not as easily acknowledged by everyone involved. In meetings, for instance, interpersonal violence occurred regularly on the cultural and mental realms. Folks on all sides of the challenge quickly interrupted each other and used judgment and blame to cow their opponents into silence. They did not label this behavior as a type of violence, instead insisting it was a necessary and appropriate response to the structural violence they perceived. Some employees were afraid to speak up because they had witnessed colleagues being shamed repeatedly for mistakes they had made months ago, no matter how much they had worked to correct the behavior. Intrapersonal violence was also high, with frequent experiences of shame, self-blame, and self-judgment as a response to any feedback, no matter how gently offered. The only type of violence that had not yet taken place was violence on the physical dimension. Working with this company required

	Intrapersonal	Interpersonal	Institutional/ Structural
Mental	Mindless consumption. Checked out.	Threats. Fear. Reduced stimuli.	Restricted access to intellectual stimulation.
Emotional	Hopelessness. Aloneness.	Myth of independence. Myth of differences.	Devaluation of certain values and practices. Appropriation. Erasure.
Spiritual-Cultural	Guilt. Shame. Put-downs.	Judgment. Blame.	Dehumanization.
Physical	Addictive behaviors. Self-harm. Neglect.	Abuse (e.g., physical, sexual). Coercion.	War. Genocide. Destruction of natural resources. Denial of access.

FIGURE 2. **Types of Violence**

© Mireille van Bremen and Roxy Manning

raising awareness of the different forms violence could take and the transformation of their ways of operating in all three spheres—intrapersonal, interpersonal, and structural.

As we can see, violence occurs in so many aspects of our lives. Once we are able to recognize this, we can begin cultivating the capacity to meet our needs while holding care for the needs of others. What can we do to respond to violence in a way that honors all our values—care for our physical, emotional, mental, and spiritual well-being—and also moves us toward a Beloved Community that creates the conditions where that care is extended and available to all? Many of us respond to violence reflexively. When we experience violence, we push back. When I teach my series on how to respond to microaggressions, one idea that I must always address is the belief that if we don't speak up or say something, we might be seen as consenting to or agreeing with what is happening. We jump into the fray and respond before we even begin the assessment I believe is necessary in order to respond with care for all and in ways that don't also result in self-violence.

Imagine that someone took actions that resulted in a host of unmet needs for you. Maybe you're feeling angry? Hurt? Hopeless? How do you respond? As I mentioned, many of us respond reflexively. Take a moment to think of what your habitual response is when someone shares a racist joke when talking to you. Some of us respond immediately with anger, attacking the person. We might attack their character, ethics, and integrity. Maybe we identify them as racist. Others might immediately withdraw. Perhaps we withdraw physically, walking away, refusing to engage further. Or we might check out mentally. Nodding politely but no longer truly engaged or interested in what the person is saying. What's your habitual response?

I believe it's essential to move from habit to intentional choice in how we respond in these situations. Sometimes our habitual response is spot-on. It's the response we would choose even with reflection. Or we might regret our habitual response. Maybe we walk away but spend the next week beating ourselves up for not advocating for ourselves and speaking up for what we value. Or maybe we cussed out the Actor (the person whose actions impacted us) but are now regretting the high cost of doing so as we face being fired from our job. Our action in response to racism and injustice is rarely either fully aligned with our values or completely ineffective. Believing it could be right or wrong would mean falling prey to dualistic thinking.

Instead, it's important to assess how well our actions actually meet our needs. When we cussed out that person, what needs did it meet? Authenticity. Self-expression. Transparency about my values. Acknowledging impact. Clarity about my boundaries. But what needs did it *not* meet? Predictability about my capacity to keep myself housed and fed. Care for others. Clarity of expression. Hope for change. It might be that when we consider this map of needs met and unmet, we might decide we were satisfied with our response. "Hey. I've put up with this environment in which I've experienced slurs and racism for so long. I can no longer keep focusing on my sustainability at the expense of my dignity and self-care. I'd rather they know how I feel and what my boundaries are because I can't keep working here under these conditions anyway. I've been getting sick dealing with the emotional stress of these repeated microaggressions, so something needs to change."

Or maybe we realize the cost was too high and wish we had

responded differently. "Hmm. I feel better not keeping that in again and again, but I'm really concerned about my job now. I wanted them to understand that those kinds of jokes are unacceptable. But I need this job. And I really want them to understand why those jokes are so painful. I don't want to have to talk to them about it, but I worry that my yelling back puts me at risk, doesn't change anything, and definitely doesn't get them to be curious about my experience."

Only when we are able to move from habit to a full understanding of what's important to us do we have the direction we need to take action that is truly supportive. Chapter 4 looks at some of the ways our brains function that could impede our capacity to operate with full choice, aligned with our dearest values.

NOTES

1. Martin Luther King Jr., " 'When Peace Becomes Obnoxious'," Martin Luther King Jr. Research and Education Institute, Stanford University, May 24, 2021, https://kinginstitute.stanford.edu/king-papers /documents/when-peace-becomes-obnoxious.

2. King, " 'When Peace Becomes Obnoxious'."

3. Marshall B. Rosenberg, *Nonviolent Communication: A Language of Life,* 3rd ed. (Encinitas, CA: PuddleDancer Press, 2015), 16.

4. "FNS—Elder Teachings by Napos," University of Wisconsin–Green Bay, February 28, 2011, https://youtu.be/LK5Et8MJJJA. "Medicine Ways: Traditional Healers and Healing," U.S. National Library of Medicine, National Institutes of Health, https://www .nlm.nih.gov/nativevoices/exhibition/healing-ways/medicine-ways /medicine-wheel.html (accessed October 2022).

4

Bias: Distortions That Disconnect

Every summer when I was in elementary school, my local library in Harlem's Washington Heights held a contest to motivate kids to read. My kids have been in similar programs. In the ones they participated in, every child would receive a prize, varying in desirability based on how many books they read. When I was a child, every kid received a certificate or sticker, but the prize—I don't even recall the specific prize now—went to the kids who read the most books. I was a fast and voracious reader who never needed an extrinsic reason to read. In fact, since I was struggling to fit in with my peers, who didn't know what to make of my bookish, shy, immigrant self, I spent my summers secluded in the house, reading for countless hours each day. I decided I would win the prize.

We were asked to complete a log listing the titles of the books we had read. After two weeks I turned in my logs naming forty books. The librarian looked at the log then at me. She asked skeptically, "Did you really read all these books?" I assured her I did. I could finish many of the short fairy tales or chapter books in an hour or two, but there were a few longer books from authors I loved, like Lucy Maud Montgomery. The librarian questioned me about the books, randomly selecting titles from the list and asking me to tell her what the book was about. I easily answered every question she asked because I really had read all the books, but I was shaking from fear that she wouldn't believe me, that I would be deemed a liar. The librarian took my logs and told me to come back later. When I returned, I was told that although they did believe me, the librarians decided not to give me the prize. Because the program was meant to encourage reluctant readers, they explained, it would not be fair for those children to compete against me. I was devastated.

When I've shared this story, a lot of adults have been outraged that the library simply didn't award two prizes that summer. They experience it as a lack of integrity that the librarians went back on their promised award because I didn't fit the mold. I remember being upset that I didn't get the prize, but a part of me rationalized it away. After reflection, my young self decided the library couldn't afford multiple prizes and agreed it really wasn't fair to other kids. At the time, I was much more impacted by the librarian's initial disbelief that I had read all the books on my list. My young self felt humiliated standing there, answering questions to prove I had read the forty books. What made them assume I was lying? Was it because I was a child and they didn't believe I would have the focus and drive to do so? Was it because I was a Black kid living in impoverished Washington Heights, and the white librarians couldn't imagine someone with my passion and aptitude for reading lived in that neighborhood?

I didn't have words for it then, but the experience of being doubted, of being met with suspicion and having my integrity questioned, was one of my earliest examples of being impacted by others' assumptions and bias.

When I was younger, each time I experienced that kind of bias, I would return to the question "Why me?" Why would someone look at me and assume I couldn't read that many books or was cheating on my paper, that I couldn't pay for the lipstick at the drug store or that they needed to explain medical concepts to me in simple language? Over time, I began to answer myself: "They're being racist." But that answer was never enough. I would then ask, "But don't they see me? Can't they tell that I'm smart...honest...educated?" At best, with that follow-up question I was asking, "What's wrong with me that I'm not giving off the signs that would help them see past my race and see all of my capabilities and skills. Sadly, I was really asking, "But can't you see I'm different than other Black folks?" with all the internalized racism and bias inherent in that question.

The answer that people make assumptions because they are racist is only part of the picture, because only some people are overtly racist. Well-intentioned people who abhor acting in consciously racist ways still make similar assumptions that lead to actions that are demonstrably biased. This happens because they are human beings who have been raised in heavily stratified societies replete with stories about other human beings. These narratives about people and groups, like the white supremacy narrative, impact the decisions we make, both consciously and unconsciously, in part because of how our brains work.

Cognitive Bias

The human brain is designed to help us efficiently process and respond to incoming stimuli. It's commonly reported that our brains process over eleven million bits of information per second, 220,000 times more than the fifty bits we can actually process consciously.[1] Think about what happens when your computer is trying to run too many programs at once. It slows down and eventually might crash. Our brains need a way to deal with the tsunami of incoming information, sort out what's important and what can be ignored, and make decisions. We develop unconscious rules called heuristics that allow us to create shortcuts in this process.

When we make decisions based on these shortcuts, we can assess how well the heuristics integrate incoming data. Some shortcuts might systematically ignore information that can be helpful. In those moments the difference between what's optimal given all the available information and what we do based on the shortcuts our brains take can be considered cognitive bias. Over the past two decades a substantial amount of scholarship has examined the notion of *race* itself as a human invention, a heuristic tool to easily—and too simplistically—categorize human beings without acknowledging the many ways these categories serve to consciously and unconsciously justify biases that have powerful material consequences.[2]

Some of these unconscious biases and shortcuts that human brains regularly use contribute to racism, even in people who consciously are deeply committed to equity and antiracist practices, and even in people who are themselves the target of racism. I'll describe a few well-researched unconscious biases that aren't necessarily or specifically about race and discuss how these shortcuts manifest in interactions around race.

Confirmation Bias

We're more likely to seek out, pay attention to, and believe information that matches or confirms the things we already believe.

One day I was walking home in the upstate New York town where I lived at the time. Suddenly two officers stopped me and hostilely questioned me. I was alarmed but answered all their questions until they let me go. As I was leaving, I asked why I was stopped. They stated a Black man had robbed a store in the neighborhood, so they were questioning likely suspects. This is an example of confirmation bias at work. The officers paid attention to the things that confirmed for them I could be a suspect: Black and large. In paying attention to only those things while deciding to approach and question me, they ignored all the physical signs that would be congruent with a cisgender woman who thus did *not* match the description of the robber in favor of those that matched their beliefs that my dark skin made me a viable suspect.

Representative Heuristic

We more readily believe something is true when it matches a model or belief we have in our mind.

A Black friend once shared how scared and angry she was after her father's visit to the DMV. Her elderly father's vision had deteriorated to the point that he was no longer able to drive safely. A former PhD chemist, he was a brilliant man who quite firmly resisted all his family's attempts to take his car keys away. Once my friend realized her father needed to renew his license, she felt relieved that he would not be able to pass the vision exam. As predicted, he was unable to read the items on the vision test. Imagine my friend's dismay when the examiner winked at him and said, "I'll pass you. I know you don't know how to read." The examiner's mental model of an elderly Black man as uneducated made it much easier for her to believe that he could not read at all than to believe he was a highly educated person whose poor vision prevented him from seeing the letters on an eye chart.

Illusory Truth Effect

When information is repeated over and over again, we tend to believe that it's true.

We may all have a strong sense of the stunning ways this phenomenon has played out politically when we consider the ease with which various conspiracy theories and fake news proliferate after copious repetition. This cognitive bias also shows up when we talk about group bias and stereotypes. In the middle of writing this book, I watched a lot of Netflix while completing a medical treatment that required me to spend hours in a confined chamber. Even though the representation of Global Majority people in media has increased and become a bit more nuanced, my recent experience shows me it's still far from enough.

Over and over again, I saw stereotypes that have been endlessly shown on that medium—the lazy and/or criminal Black man, the industrious and weak Asian character, the Middle Eastern folks plotting to bring down the West, the undocumented South American immigrant, the strong Black woman who supports everyone around her at high cost to herself. As these stereotypes are repeatedly offered for the public's consumption, it's no wonder that they have become part of the mental model that so many people hold of these groups. And sadly, because of the constant repetition, people will believe they are true. Research has shown that people continue to use and reference misinformation even after they acknowledge receiving new information and say they understand that the old information was retracted![3]

Group Attribution Error

We believe that the behavior of someone from a group we don't belong to is typical of all members of that group.

One challenging impact of racism I've heard from so many people from the Global Majority is the result of this cognitive bias. Frederick Harris discusses the impact of respectability politics, "a philosophy promulgated by black elites to 'uplift the race' by correcting the 'bad' traits of the black poor in the Black community," and thus gain approval and support from white people.[4] Harris notes that while respectability politics was one of several effective strategies that helped some members of the Black community, its focus on personal responsibility often ignores, and in fact has at times explicitly discounted, the impact of racist social institutions.[5]

This philosophy left so many Black folks terrified of doing anything that would reinforce racist stereotypes. Women are afraid of expressing anger because they don't want to be seen as the angry Black woman. A beloved elder sobbed as he recounted the relentless pressure he had internalized and conformed to his entire life to always appear perfect—perfect dress, grooming, speech, diction, home—all so he would not discredit the race. I remember how self-conscious I became about my speech when I realized the malapropisms I sometimes uttered might be seen by white colleagues as more proof of the inferior education of Black folks.

Availability Bias

The more easily we can remember something happening in the past, the greater the likelihood we think it will happen again.

We might not even be remembering something that happened to us. We talked earlier about how the simple repetitions of stereotyped depictions in the media contribute to people's ideas that those stereotypes are true. The availability bias amplifies that impact since the more people encounter those stereotypes, even fictionally, the easier it is to remember them. As a child growing up in Harlem, I never saw someone get shot or even held up. When I went to college, a friend from Virginia came to visit me. She had never been to Harlem but had seen countless movies about gang violence in Harlem. She was terrified to walk the streets in my neighborhood, convinced that the memories she had of seeing violence in Harlem depicted in movies and on news stories made her predictions that she could be robbed or hurt every time we left the house likely, despite my assuring her that this had never happened to me.

Headwind/Tailwind Bias

We are more likely to remember challenges (headwinds) that we worked hard to overcome and to forget privileges (tailwinds) we enjoyed that smoothed our way.[6]

Researchers Shai Davidai and Thomas Gilovich identified a specific subtype of the availability bias —the headwind/tailwind bias—that can contribute to one of the ways dialogues about racism unfold. Several times when I've announced that reduced tuition was available to attend one of my classes especially for people from the Global Majority, I've fielded calls from angry white people who accused me of not acknowledging the many challenges so many white people have to overcome. One woman who called spoke at length about the degree of poverty and trauma she experienced in childhood as she asked me to change my policy. While clarifying if she had a request for support, I learned she was financially stable—the result of receiving support from adults who encouraged her, helped her apply for scholarships, and recommended her to jobs. She had ignored all the support she benefited from and focused only on the challenges she had overcome as she used herself to make her case for me not to name race and ethnicity as one of the criteria for the scholarship.

In-Group Bias

We tend to prefer and give privileges to people we think belong to the same group as us.

The in-group bias is quite strong and easily activated. Researchers have found that even made-up affiliations—like telling participants that someone they had never met before liked the same thing they did—led the participants to offer more money to those they thought were similar to themselves than to those they thought were not. We see in-group bias show up in numerous everyday interactions. Imagine walking into a gathering where you don't know anyone. How do you choose the person with whom you'll speak? Do you walk toward the person wearing something with a logo from a team you like? Do you smile at a person who like you has a book in their hand, or maybe notice the person with a sticker on their water bottle? Many of us begin unconsciously focusing on signs that someone is a member of one of our groups in these situations.

Since the brain's use of these and other heuristics often results in unwanted bias in our interactions and decision making, must we simply accept that bias is a necessary part of the human condition? What hope can we have of building an antiracist society that is closer to our vision of Beloved Community? In fact, knowing about cognitive biases is an essential step toward that vision. A friend, Steve, shared that once he became aware of the strength of his in-group bias, he began to work actively to combat it. Whenever he noticed that his brain was unconsciously steering him away from certain people, he deliberately chose to interact with them.

In her book *The End of Bias: A Beginning*, Jessica Nordell describes numerous studies and real-world interventions demonstrating that when we become aware of our cognitive biases, we can redesign our systems and structures to combat them.[7] My eldest completed his master's degree in political science in the UK. He was surprised to discover that in every one of his classes, student work had to be turned in with no identifying information on it. This anonymous work was then graded by someone selected from a pool of instructors. Despite decades of research showing biases in how student work is evaluated, he had never experienced a grading system so well designed to structurally reduce some of those biases. When we acknowledge how our brains work and that bias exists, we can create systems to remove bias that are designed to overcome the brain's tendencies.

An effective way to work with some of our built-in cognitive biases is to be rigorous about how we describe the world around us and our experience of it. How we talk about what we experience is key. One of my clients discussed an experience that was painful for him. Tomás is a dark brown–skinned South American immigrant working for a large company; he believed his new manager was unfairly policing his work. Tomás accompanied his supervisor, Cara, to meet with a client while his colleagues were working on a deadline back at the office. During the meeting, Tomás received several texts from the colleagues asking for a time-sensitive report. As he was texting to clarify the information he needed to send, Cara leaned over and said with some energy in her voice: "Be professional." A bit confused, Tomás looked at her then continued working. As Tomás opened his laptop to send the files while continuing to text with his colleagues, Cara leaned over again and said in a sharp tone of voice: "Pay attention. Do your personal stuff on your own time." Cara's erroneous conclusion likely emerged from several cognitive biases operating simultaneously. Tomás experienced Cara's tense remark as stemming from a racist stereotype that did not acknowledge Tomás's extensive history of competence and professionalism.

Numerous media depictions of Black and Brown men as

shiftless and unprofessional may have contributed to Cara holding an internalized belief that these media stereotypes were true via the illusory truth effect. Since she could easily pull up instances in her memory of unprofessional men of color, the availability heuristic would make it more likely Cara would predict unprofessional behavior was happening again. Confirmation bias would then lead Cara to look for the evidence that matched her belief that Tomás was unprofessional (he was on his phone and laptop during a work meeting, he appeared distracted from the topic being discussed) and forget or discard evidence that would counter that belief (Cara's knowledge that there was a deadline at the office and that Tomás was the holder of information relevant to meeting that deadline).

The Role of Observations

In the previous anecdote, what could Cara have done to counter this confluence of cognitive biases? One key step for someone who is aware of the human brain's tendency to leap to biased conclusions is to slow down and separate their observations from their interpretations. We want to start a conversation by being clear about what is being observed. When we make observations, we may increase our chances that we can engage in productive dialogue about an issue. Many communication approaches talk about the importance of making observations. I've often heard true observations defined as a description of what's happening in the environment that everyone would agree upon. Some people use the video camera as an example, stating a true observation is "what a video camera can record."

However, this perspective perpetuates the myth of the

neutral, unbiased observer and can actually contribute to the continuation of racist inequities. Video cameras are placed in a specific location, with a specific quality of lens pointed in a specific direction, to record a stimulus determined by the operator. There is considerable choice in where the operator places the camera, when they turn it on and off, who it is pointed at, and what filters are placed on the lens. What is recorded by the video camera thus inherently reflects the operator's choices and biases. When we promote the idea of objective observations without even including who the observer is or acknowledging other perspectives, we promote one person's or group's experience as the objectively true one over all the others that we don't acknowledge.

Remember confirmation bias? If I gave one hundred people cameras and asked them to record an event, confirmation bias would suggest that people would selectively attend to and record things that confirm whatever beliefs they have about the event. Following the murder of George Floyd, there were many protests against racism and anti-Black policies throughout the United States. Despite thousands of people marching peacefully, what was recorded and displayed varied widely. Reporting on some news channels and media outlets by people aligned with the marchers' goals often showed footage of hundreds of folks marching peacefully, listening to speeches, or engaging in call-and-response with speakers. News reports on several national news stations that were opposed to the marchers' stance seemed only to display footage of violent interactions and looted or damaged property. We cannot assume that what is recorded or observed is not biased. We also cannot assume that even when most sources show the same recording or a majority of people say they witnessed the same thing, what is reported captures the totality of everything that happened. It's therefore helpful to attach the observation to the person or group reporting that observation since the observer becomes as much a part of the description of what is occurring as the event itself.

Why do we want to make observations then, if they inherently reflect a person's perspective and assumptions? When I share my observations, I share what I perceive, knowing it may be different from what you experience. I own my observations as mine and can be curious about what's missing from my experience. If I shared my interpretations, you may be so focused on challenging a description you believe is off the mark that you don't acknowledge the underlying need stimulated by my interpretation that is prompting me to speak. If you hear my observations, you may more clearly see the needs that the observation stimulated than if you heard only my interpretations. When we share our observations of an interaction or event, we are able to slow down and check in about each of our perceptions and the meaning we are attributing to them, rather than accept that meaning as truth.

I've expanded on the traditional framing of observations used by such approaches as Nonviolent Communication to describe more fully the different ways we can experience an event. Nonviolent Communication proposes that when an event occurs, we interpret it as contributing to our needs being met or not being met. This leads to our reactions to and feelings about that event. This frame allows us to move from a stance of objective truth that contributes to right-wrong thinking to one of inquiry about how a stimulus is contributing to impact. If we understand what the stimulus is, we can begin to better make sense of a person's reactions by

Observation Iceberg

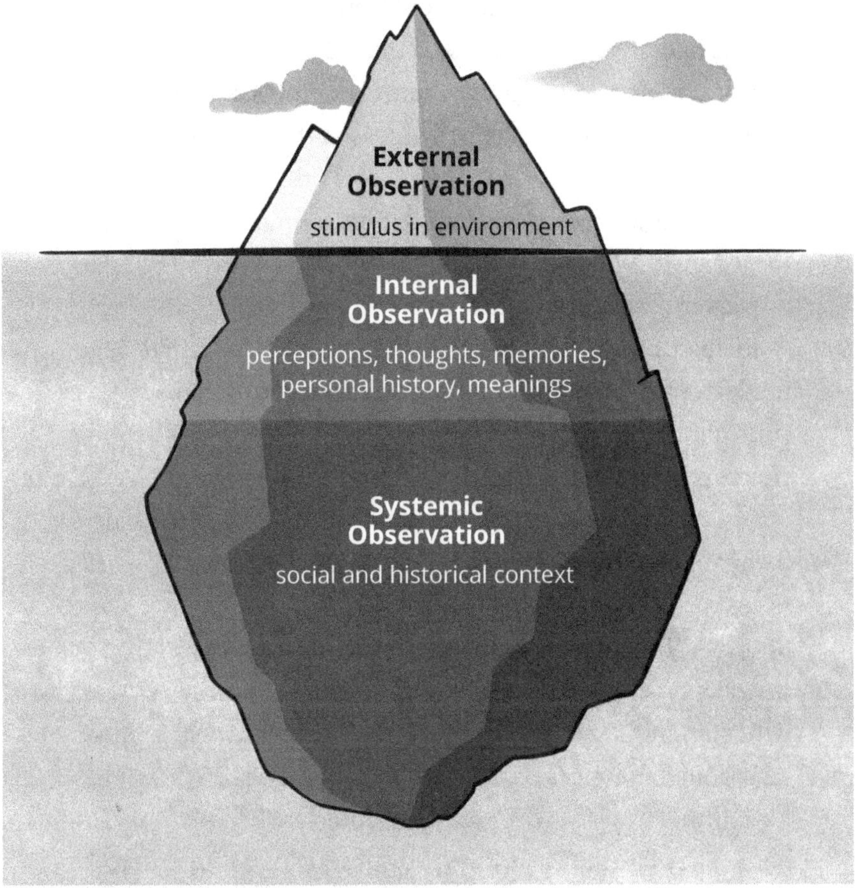

FIGURE 3. Levels of Observations
© Mireille van Bremen and Roxy Manning

discerning how they understand the stimulus contributes to meeting their needs. To fully understand the different ways awareness of our needs can be stimulated by events around us, I developed the Observation Iceberg, which describes three levels at which observations can occur (Figure 3).

External Observations

When Cara leaned over and told Tomás to be professional, Tomás had no idea why she said that. Cara's words conveyed her judgment that Tomás was acting unprofessionally but offered no clue about what she witnessed that led her to make that judgment. When we make external observations, we describe what we are perceiving that others might also be able to perceive. We acknowledge something occurring outside ourselves that is stimulating us.

Instead of leading with her judgment, Cara could have made the following external observation: "I saw you were on your computer and texting during our meeting." With this clear external observation, Tomás would have a clear sense of what Cara was reacting to. Similarly, Tomás was upset when he heard Cara's judgments. If he wanted to talk to her about his experience, he might share his external observation: "You told me, 'Be professional' and then said, 'Pay attention. Do your personal stuff on your own time' when I was interacting with staff in the home office who requested my help to meet an urgent deadline."

External observations are represented as the tip of the iceberg. They are the easiest level of observations for others to share. However, external observations might vary between people since factors like prior experience, capacity in the moment, and cognitive biases all impact what we perceive and thus what external observation we make. Even if we don't take in the full observation, someone else who is present might point out what we missed since a stimulus occurring outside of us may be perceived by more than one person. Cara only took in one level of external observation—Tomás's texting and use of the computer. However, when Tomás points out the other external observations—the requests for help from home office staff, the urgent deadline, and the context of the texts he had sent—Cara would be able to perceive them as well.

Generally, only a small fraction of the mass of an iceberg is visible above water even though the larger mass underneath can cause significant damage to ships. Likewise with observations, the parts we can see and agree upon—the external observations—represent only a small part of what is happening that can stimulate so much emotion in a given situation. Recognizing these other levels can bring us humility when we believe that someone is "overreacting" and lead to curiosity about what else may be going on beyond what we have perceived.

Internal Observations

The external layer triggers the internal reaction, often automatically without our intentional choice. Internal observations are our perception of what happens inside ourselves in response to the external observations. We can observe the memories, implicit associations, physical sensations, and meanings that are stimulated by the external events.

Earlier I described two interactions I had with the police—being stopped under suspicion of being someone who had robbed a store and having the police stop our car and talk with my (white) friend privately to be sure he wasn't being kidnapped. The next time I saw police lights in my rearview mirror, I had an immediate reaction—I began shaking and crying. I was terrified. If I were to describe only the external observation—"I saw a police car pull behind me and its lights turned on, signaling me to pull over"—you might not understand why I felt terrified. Someone else in the same situation might be frustrated when they saw the lights, perhaps because they really wanted to get to work on time. Without the internal observation, I am likely to be less understandable to others. If you add the internal observation, you would be more likely to guess what my needs were. My internal observation might be, "I noticed I was shaking and crying and then I remembered being stopped by the police twice because they thought I had committed a crime." Hearing that, my terror might become understandable. You could imagine my longing for safety and freedom, even if it were not what would be stimulated for you.

Although we might guess, we never truly know someone else's internal observation until they tell us. We have no way of knowing what sensations, memories, or associations are triggered for someone in any situation. Knowing about internal observations invites us to be curious when someone is responding to a situation in a way that's markedly different than we might expect. Let's see how that might work in the situation with Cara and Tomás. Tomás had a strong negative reaction to Cara telling him to "be professional" and "do personal stuff on your own time." The words alone do not explain Tomás's reaction. I've seen coworkers who were reprimanded for doing personal things, shrug it off, and quietly keep doing what they were doing. In this case, Tomás's history helps explain his reaction. He described experiencing a sinking feeling in his stomach and recalling multiple occasions in which his behavior was misconstrued by supervisors and peers. When Cara spoke to Tomás this time, those memories came flooding back. He felt angry and hopeless since he so longed to be seen for his contributions and professionalism.

Systemic Observations

When an event happens, we are impacted not just by its associations with our personal histories but also by its associations to the larger social contexts in which the event occurs. Just like our internal observations can arise automatically, so too can our systemic observations. This is another place where our cognitive biases come into play. When Cara looked over and saw Tomás texting, it's likely that her brain drew on numerous instances of men of the Global Majority slacking off at work, perhaps depicted routinely in television shows and movies. Despite these depictions being false, Cara's brain encoded them and they were readily available to be activated as fact. Even though Cara would explicitly say she does not believe this stereotype, the unconscious activation of it by the external stimuli would impact her understanding and reaction. Her exasperation with Tomás is greater than one might have expected given this was her first time ever seeing him text during a meeting. Instead, what she might have experienced in that moment was the external observation of seeing Tomás text during a meeting combined with the activation of stereotypes encoded in her brain of men of the Global Majority being lazy. It is this observation combined with the results of cognitive bias that contributed to the depth of Cara's frustration.

Similarly, when Tomás heard Cara's words, he likely had some systemic observations activated. Tomás has heard numerous stories of supervisors policing the behavior of Global Majority folks. He is aware of the many studies that show bias against Global Majority people in the workplace. As he heard Cara speak, it stimulated not just his memories of not being seen for his work, but his understanding of the extent to which this lack of acknowledgment is a pattern that is experienced by people like him. His frustration and hopelessness was likely compounded with a sense of the current experience being a pervasive one that has resulted in so much harm for so many other people beyond him.

Cognitive biases impact our external observations by constraining the stimuli we take in. They also impact our internal and systemic observations by activating memories and beliefs that live in us beyond our conscious awareness. The connection to our past experiences and schemas when they are painful means that we are often experiencing an increase in pain. That is, not just the present moment pain but that of the past adds to the overall stimulation. Similarly, when the stimulus is pleasurable, the connection to past experiences and beliefs may add to our overall stimulation in the moment, causing us to experience a more intensified sense of pleasure than the actual stimulus might otherwise warrant.

If we pause to witness and name our external, internal, and systemic observations, we create a space in which we can question them and the conclusions they bring. Instead of speaking the judgments, Cara might choose to notice them and use them as a signal to rewind and check her observations. Doing so might lead her to realize that systemic stereotypes she is working to free herself from were activated for her and that she has always seen Tomás act professionally, contrary to those stereotypes. This might lead her to ask for a five-minute break in the meeting and privately say to Tomás:

"Tomás, I saw you are texting and using your laptop during our meeting with the client. It's not signaling to the client that they are our top focus while we're meeting with them and I'm feeling frustrated. Can you share what you were working on so we can figure out how to prioritize things in the future?"

If Cara did speak sharply to Tomás and he wants to share how he was impacted, Tomás can describe his experience using all three levels of observation so that Cara could take in the full impact: "When you told me 'Pay attention. Do your personal stuff on your own time,' while I was sending texts attending to our team's priorities, I was reminded of other times when supervisors jumped to conclusions that I was not doing my work. And it brought up for me how often this happens to Global Majority people like me and can even lead to us being fired. I feel incredibly worried about my job security and frustrated and hopeless because I so want to be trusted for my integrity, and to know I work in an organization that is freeing itself from patterns that have harmed and continue to harm people like me."

As we work toward building Beloved Community where all human beings thrive, understanding the brain's functioning can protect us against some of the barriers toward that goal. It would be easy for Cara to fall into shame if she observes the easily activated stereotype or even, sadly, to double down on her judgment. Instead, if we can hold that all of us have to work rigorously to recognize and transform those stereotypes and biases when they emerge, we can question our assumptions when they arise and we can invite in other perspectives. It would be easy for Tomás to respond to the deep frustration and pain he feels after hearing Cara's words by giving up and writing her off as racist. If instead he is able to slow down and notice what's coming up for him and speak it fully, Tomás is able to help both himself and Cara contextualize why her words were so impactful. This creates the possibility that Tomás's authentic expression can set the stage for Cara to realign her words and actions to match how she wants to be in the world.

We've seen how many forms of cognitive biases impact our ability to take in information and see the world as it truly is, even when we are trying to do so. As multiple forms of bias interact and amplify each other, they lead our view of the world to diverge from that of those exposed to different information than we are. Understanding the relationship between bias and what we take in and understand about the world can support our humility about the truth of our experience and invite our curiosity into others' experience. In Chapter 5 we'll begin exploring how to connect over these and other differences.

NOTES

1. "Understanding Unconscious Bias," *Shortwave*, NPR, aired July 15, 2020, https://www.npr.org/2020/07/14/891140598/understanding-unconscious-bias.

2. Carol C. Mukhopadhyay, Rosemary Henze, and Yolanda T. Moses, *How Real Is Race?: A Sourcebook on Race, Culture, and Biology*, 2nd ed. (Lanham, MD: Rowman & Littlefield Publishers, 2013). A great exploration on the invention of race is Christine Herbes-Sommers, Tracy Heather Strain, and Llewellyn Smith, dirs., *Race: The Power of an Illusion* (San Francisco, CA: California Newsreel, 2003), https://www.racepowerofanillusion.org/.

3. Stephan Lewandowsky, Ullrich K. Ecker, Colleen M. Seifert, Norbert Schwarz, and John Cook, "Misinformation and Its Correction: Continued Influence and Successful Debiasing," *Psychological Science in*

the Public Interest 13, no. 3 (September 17, 2012): 106–31, https://doi.org /10.1177/1529100612451018.

4. Fredrick C. Harris, "The Rise of Respectability Politics," *Dissent Magazine* (Winter 2014), https://www.dissentmagazine.org/article/the -rise-of-respectability-politics.

5. Harris, "Rise of Respectability Politics."

6. Shai Davidai and Thomas Gilovich, "The Headwinds/Tailwinds Asymmetry: An Availability Bias in Assessments of Barriers and Blessings," *Journal of Personality and Social Psychology* 111, no. 6 (2016): 835–51, https://doi.org/10.1037/pspa0000066.

7. Jessica Nordell, *The End of Bias: A Beginning: The Science and Practice of Overcoming Unconscious Bias* (New York: Metropolitan Books, 2021).

5

Opening to Authentic Dialogue

Over the years I've witnessed and even engaged in numerous conversations that were not productive. One of the trainers from whom I first learned Nonviolent Communication was a Global Majority person who integrated an awareness of power and privilege in their work and inspired me deeply. I was determined to support them whenever possible and brought them in to work on other projects with me. Over time, I was dismayed to realize that despite our shared passion for an antiracist lens in Nonviolent Communication teaching and our shared identity as Global Majority people, we often experienced conflict.

I grew increasingly upset as our workstyles didn't match, from little issues like being on time to meetings, to larger issues such as how to share expenses and income. As our conflict grew, I attempted several times to talk about our challenges, but those attempts often ended with me listening while they expressed themselves. I finally requested a facilitated dialogue to connect and come up with agreements about working together. Unfortunately, by the time that conversation happened, this colleague and I were both in so much distress about the relationship that it devolved into each of us trying to prove that the other was wrong. We never worked together or spoke after that conversation. Had I known that different kinds of dialogues were possible, I would have approached our interactions quite differently.

Those unproductive conversations with my colleague demonstrate several places where dialogue often fails. Initially I was afraid to speak honestly with them about how I was impacted by their not following through with agreements or the demands they were making to support their goals. When I finally mustered the courage to share how I was feeling about our relationship, I did so without full awareness of what I wanted out of that conversation. We often don't know, even deep within ourselves, why we're seeking dialogue. Without that clarity, we can't ask for what we really need. When we engage in Authentic Dialogue, we aim to do so with clarity on three elements:

- Am I truly seeking dialogue?
- Why is this dialogue important to me?
- What am I seeking from the other person?

Without an understanding of these pieces, there's a good chance that the conversation we seek to have will at best be unproductive and at worst lead to greater disconnection like mine did.

I asked several people to tell me what comes up for them when they hear the phrase "We need to talk." One person captured the almost universal sentiment. He immediately thinks: "Uh oh. Someone wants to tell me what I did that they're upset about." For many people this phrase doesn't suggest a conversation is about to begin—in fact, there's often very little dialogue occurring in conversations initiated by this phrase. We don't expect true dialogue—an exchange with the goal of connection and mutual understanding—will happen. Instead, we might believe we will need to listen while someone vents at us, then find a way to appease the person who is upset.

Therefore, before asking for a dialogue, we need to reflect on our readiness for a true exchange focused on mutual understanding. Do we have the internal spaciousness and capacity to hear the other person? Are we ready to fully express our truth? Do we have clarity on why we're even requesting a conversation with that specific person? There are many reasons why we might initiate a conversation, each drawing on different skills from the participants. As the situation with my colleague unfolded, my reason for wanting to talk with them changed, even though how I approached the conversation unfortunately did not.

Reasons for Asking for Connection with Another Person

To Establish a Solution

When in conflict, we might ask to have a dialogue in the hopes of finding a solution to the conflict. In an ideal world the expectation is that after speaking, everyone involved will be able to arrive at a solution that works for all. Each person can describe what's important for them in the conflict and what needs must be addressed. Then, through brainstorming, we can arrive at a solution that would attend to the greatest set of needs.

Even when this purpose for dialogue is quite clear, we might experience roadblocks as we attempt to reach a solution.

Sometimes we need to choose a different type of dialogue to build enough trust and connection between the parties so that a viable solution can be reached. We might start with self-reflection, or we can ask a trusted friend for empathy—a process in which they listen to us and reflect our feelings, needs, and values to help us understand more explicitly what is stimulating us. Several times when I asked my colleague to talk, I did so in response to an interaction between us that had been so distressing to me that I overrode my tendency for conflict avoidance. I always convinced myself in those moments that we had to talk to fix whatever was not working. Without really taking the time to understand why I was upset, I often tried to fix the surface problems without attending to the deeper ones. After waiting more than an hour for them to arrive at a meeting, I tried to talk with them to come up with strategies to ensure meetings would start on time. We came up with multiple ideas—morning instead of afternoon start times, setting a window rather than a specific start time, contacting each other when we were on the way to the meeting. But I never acknowledged my general overwhelm, even to myself, that was greater than our relationship itself.

As a stay-at-home parent with three young ones, I was overcommitted in trying to manage my household while also attending to all that was involved in putting on multiple retreats and programs each year. My anger was only partly at the late start. Instead, had I requested empathic support before the solution conversation, I might have recognized that I really needed to set a limit to how often I would meet, how long I would wait, or even if I wanted to work on the project at this time in my life—things completely under my control. The answers to those questions could have shifted, and perhaps

Ask yourself:	If NO, consider these actions:
• Am I clear on what's important to me in this situation?	> Get self-empathy or empathy.
• Am I open to hearing the other person's experience and perspective in this dialogue?	> Get self-empathy or empathy. Request a dialogue **TO BE HEARD**. Request a dialogue **FOR HEALING**.
• Do I have clarity on all the factors that are contributing to the situation?	> Request a dialogue **FOR SHARED UNDERSTANDING**.
• Do I believe there are other perspectives on the problem worth considering?	> Request a dialogue **FOR SHARED UNDERSTANDING**.
• Do I believe there may be multiple solutions to the issue?	> Get self-empathy or empathy and then decide which dialogue to request.

FIGURE 4. Assessing Readiness for Solution Conversations
© Mireille van Bremen and Roxy Manning

even negated, the need for strategies for meetings I was not truly wanting.

Figure 4 offers a set of questions, a decision flow chart, that can help you determine if you are really ready for and wanting a solution-focused conversation.

To Create Shared Understanding

Another purpose for dialogue is to determine if everyone involved is holding the same perspective on the issue. Many factors can contribute to a difference in perspective. Each person holds information about their experience and motivations that influences how they understand what is important. We often assume that our perspective is shared by the other. Without explicitly checking, however, we run the risk of overlooking significant gaps in understanding. Conversations for shared understanding can identify where more information is needed so that decisions and actions can emerge from the same place.

After several meetings with this same colleague in which I was frustrated when we did not follow the agreed-upon agenda, I kept trying to get us to agree on strategies to get more clarity about the agenda before we met. Instead, I could have asked for a conversation to check for congruence of our goals. I might have shared my understanding that we were working as equal partners to design and deliver a strong program with quality content and that I was overwhelmed holding most of the logistical load. My colleague might have shared that they prioritized surfacing and exploring theoretical limits of the work we were doing, and that the program provided material for that exploration. They did not see logistics as a significant part of their work and trusted that as long as we took time to explore the ideological and conceptual implications whenever they came up, the logistic pieces would be taken care of by those prioritizing them. A conversation to ensure we were each holding full awareness of the other's needs and assumptions could have shifted how we approached our part of the situation. In a conversation for shared understanding, each person enters the conversation expecting to express what is true for them and to reflect back their understanding of the other person's experience.

To Be Heard

The purpose of conversations that focus on ensuring a person is heard begins with a person sharing their experience and having the listener reflect back what is important to the sharer. This is often the type of conversation we are looking for when we say "We need to talk." The person who is sharing may want to express the full depth of their experience—anger, despair, joy, excitement—without needing to tone it down or worry how the listener might receive their words. Whether or not it is possible to change the situation, the person sharing likely wants the listener to take in and acknowledge the impact they received.

With this intention we have to decide if we want to be heard by the Actor—the person who impacted us—or if it would work for anyone to hear our experience. Sometimes the Actor isn't the best person to hear us, since they are navigating their own emotions and reactions to what happened. As they hear the full extent of our experience, they may spiral into guilt and shame. If the Actor really wants to be the one to hear us, they can choose to get support from someone else in order to stay present in the conversation. This is something I often do in such situations. In a conversation where someone is asking to be heard, if I choose to listen to them, I want to listen without a sense of judgment, defensiveness, or a specific agenda. I might need to prepare myself in order to listen so openly. While I can jump right into hearing someone's frustration about an experience that happened with a stranger, I often need some time to self-connect and prepare when I agree to listen to someone's dissatisfaction with me.

And often, as was the case with my colleague, both people have some pain and anger when there is conflict. In that case there could even be an explicit agreement for one person to be heard first without the listener sharing their experience or their intention. After the speaker has been heard, possibly at a different time, the listener would have a turn to share their experience and be heard with the same curiosity and openness about their perspective and experience. This strategy would have been hugely supportive in my interactions with my colleague. Each time we attempted to speak, we would each be so frustrated that we interrupted each other. I wasn't listening to them—my frustration blocked me from taking in and possibly being moved by their experience. Instead, confirmation bias fully activated, I was listening for the bits of information that matched my beliefs. I listened only to obtain the ammunition I needed to prove they were wrong.

There are some situations where it does not make sense to agree to be in a conversation where we will be listening to someone who wants their experience known. Sometimes we're still in too much pain ourselves. If I can't refrain from judging and blaming the other person or contesting their perspective, I can take that as a sign that I might need some support elsewhere. Before entering that last conversation with my colleague, I could have reached out to my community and asked for empathy. Someone could have listened to all that was going on for me, helping release the pressure to be heard coming out of years of conflict and helping me gain clarity on what my truth was before I attempted to listen to my colleague and share my truth with them.

We also might encounter situations where someone is blatantly contesting what we believe to be true. A commitment to Authentic Dialogue does not mandate that we must agree to talk with everyone who approaches us. It's important to assess our own capacity, willingness, and sense of efficacy when agreeing to talk. For example, my parents once fed and housed a white man who was down on his luck for several years without charging him anything. He watched movies with my dad and helped him in and out of the pool but was not expected to do much since the home health aides provided much of the support my parents needed. After meeting a new partner, the white man suddenly left the house without notifying my parents. Shortly afterward, he began posting racist messages on social media. My parents were heartbroken. After seeing several posts in which this man claimed that Black people were inferior and that he viewed my family success as the exception that proved this rule because we had Asian ancestry, I wanted to understand what had happened. When we connected, he continued to insist that there was scientific evidence supporting the inferiority of Black people. Checking in more deeply with myself, I realized I had little desire to engage further. Despite this man's attempts to continue the dialogue, I did not want to put energy into engaging with someone who not only was spouting easily disprovable claims but was also unable to acknowledge my family's care and the impact of his actions.

Engaging in Authentic Dialogues should not require that we submit to someone else's agenda with no consideration of our own, or agree that their perspective is the only true one.

It should not be a traumatizing act of submission, appeasement, and denial of our own experience. There is no demand that we stay in dialogue when there is little hope that the other person is truly interested in understanding our experience or capable of shifting. I opted not to have further contact because I did not trust this man was in a place where he truly could hear me, and it was not supportive to me to hear his narrative. I could say no out of self-care without needing to put him down to legitimize my breaking off contact. Prioritize your well-being as you decide where and with whom you want to put in the energy to do this kind of work.

If you choose a dialogue with the intention that each person will be heard, it's important to create the space for each person to express their truth and receive a reflection that demonstrates their experience was understood, even if everyone involved does not have the same external observations. This dialogue requires that each speaker enter the conversation with some understanding of what their own truth is. Each person might need to do some self-exploration or get support from friends to truly know what they want to be heard about. We might also need to explore any internal blocks that prevent us from expressing our truth. Some of us hold a belief that we're too much, that sharing our honest experience, especially when it's negative, might drive others away from us. So even when we request to be heard, we hold back from saying our full truth. In order to participate in a conversation where everyone will be heard and not drop ourselves, we need to come prepared to show up courageously, with clarity about what we want to share.

A person who agrees to show up and hear another person's experience also needs to do their own work. When we are in the listening role, we must be curious about the speaker's experience. The listener needs the capacity to take in the other person's expression and reflect back the essence of it, of what is important to the speaker. The listener needs to be able to separate their truth from the speaker's, holding the possibility of multiple truths existing, so that they can show the speaker that their reality was understood.

For Healing

Relationships can be damaged when we experience impact stimulated by someone else's actions. We might ask for a conversation whose purpose is to repair the connection. These kinds of conversations are related to the previous two types—to create shared understanding and to be heard. We often need to create space in which each person can be heard, then we can establish mutual understanding regarding what happened. Once we understand what happened and trust the impact we received is known, we can begin to address the meaning we often create to explain these situations—meanings that can lead to great pain.

With my colleague I struggled to make sense of our ongoing conflict. I worried that I was not enough. Was I not Black enough to be seen as an equal companion in the work? Was I not strong enough to prevent others from treating me as a target or victim? Was I not aware enough of self-care practices that I was being an unreasonable taskmaster instead of someone who could build community? I also worried this was another manifestation of the internalized racism that has resulted in Global Majority folks taking advantage of each other and interacting with the lack of care and respect that white supremacy thinking promotes. A part of me believed all these things were true, so my reactions to my colleague were bigger than they needed to be. I was responding not just to the specific actions they took, such as repeatedly being late or insisting on being the only one paid on a team when the rest of us had to absorb financial loss to pay them. I was also pushing back against my own insecurities and internalized oppression.

A healing conversation would require significant vulnerability. I might give voice to the doubts in my head, the ways I was making sense of their actions, and check to see if my assumptions were indeed true. As I learned more about the reasons for my colleague's actions, reasons that might have nothing to do with me, I could begin to shift the intensity of the stories of my inadequacy I was holding—and even let them go. The challenge with my colleague was never resolved as we ended our collaboration. But my judgments of them and my self-judgments did resolve as I gained more understanding of the layers in which I was impacted.

A conversation for healing works to release some of the pain we might be experiencing and to release narratives and stories that amplify that pain. It requires the speaker to be willing to speak from a place of vulnerability to create the conditions where change can happen. The speaker also needs the capacity to assess their well-being even as they speak, to know when they are no longer willing to risk potential costs to their emotional health, sustainability, belonging, and energy, among other risks. If the speaker cannot monitor their own well-being, care should be taken to be sure there is someone available who can support the speaker, checking in to see if the depth of expression is still serving them. The listener in these conversations for healing needs all of the skills from previous conversations—empathic listening skills, willing-ness to be curious, nonjudgmental stance.

The listener is also likely to need the ability to empathize with themselves, connecting to their own needs and values—to hold themselves with compassion as they might hear judg-ment and blame from the speaker. The listener must remain open to the speaker's perspective and experience, even when the speaker is telling the listener that the listener's actions have caused the speaker pain, without falling into the abyss of self-judgment and blame or throwing up huge walls to ward off the impact of hearing the speaker's experience. It's a delicate balance to keep ourselves fully open to taking in another person's experience and still hold self-compassion.

As you can see, full Authentic Dialogue starts long before we are ready to focus on the solution to a conflict. It is helpful to think of Authentic Dialogue as an iterative process—com-pleting each step will lead to an awareness and outcome that might shift how we approach future steps and might require us to go back and begin the process again. To make our con-versations most productive, we need to assess what stage we're starting from. As dialogue progresses, we may need to choose a different stage, and even return to one we thought we had completed, to work from our full power. We need to be honest with ourselves—are we truly ready to hear the other person, or do we need to be heard first? Do we have narratives or long-standing contracts (unconscious internal rules we've set for ourselves) that inhibit our full expression or limit our capacity to take in the experience of the other person?

Taking care to identify the different reasons we seek con-versation and to let the other person know what we're looking for greatly increases the chance of success with Authentic Dialogue. Instead of "We need to talk," Authentic Dialogues might start as in the following examples:

- "I would like to share some things that have been hard for me. Can you listen and reflect what you hear is true for me, even if it might be hard for you to hear?"
- "I noticed there's been some conflict between us. Are you up for checking in to see if we are on the same page about what we're expecting to contribute to this project?"
- "I'm finding our working relationship challenging and am worried that there's some internalized racism playing out for both you and me. I'd like to talk through some of the things that have happened and see if I can make sense of what's going on. Are you up for that conversation?"

When we are clear about the values and beliefs that guide our intention to connect in any situation, doing the inner work of staying tuned in to ourselves and our goals is the next part of applying the Authentic Dialogue framework, which will be explored in Chapter 6.

6

Bringing Nonviolent Communication into Authentic Dialogue

Even when we know we want to have a conversation with someone, and we're clear on *why* we want to have that conversation, we still may be unsure of the *how*. Manuela Molina, a Latina colleague, shared with me an interaction she had at a professional development workshop at an Ivy League institution. Manuela had completed a two-year program at that institution during which she took several classes with Dr. Jones, a white female faculty member. A year later, Manuela returned to complete a weeklong professional development intensive with Dr. Jones. Manuela was very aware of how important it was to make connections and develop relationships with senior figures in her field. At the start of the program's barbecue social, she watched several participants approach Dr. Jones to chat. Finally, she saw Dr. Jones was alone and approached her, excited to reconnect.

The conversation never flowed. When Manuela asked open-ended questions, Dr. Jones answered using short phrases and did not elaborate. When Manuela attempted to share a bit about her research and professional work,

Dr. Jones listened but did not respond with any follow-up questions or comments. Between each exchange, there was a pause while Manuela struggled to come up with a way to engage Dr. Jones. Dr. Jones did not initiate any questions or conversational topics. As they stood in silence, Lara, a white friend of my colleague, approached. Lara was attending the workshop but had no other connection with Dr. Jones. Dr. Jones smiled broadly at Lara. Manuela watched as Dr. Jones and Lara chatted fluidly. Dr. Jones began by asking Lara general questions—where she was from, where she was currently working—and chatting about their shared interests.

Manuela was surprised, as Dr. Jones had not asked Manuela any of these questions. As Lara talked about her work, Dr. Jones responded with compliments and shared connections with her own research. When Lara asked Dr. Jones questions, Dr. Jones answered at length, sharing stories and checking to see if Lara had any follow-up questions. Manuela was disturbed. Although she wanted to talk with Dr. Jones about the interaction, Manuela didn't trust that Dr. Jones would share the same observations of what had happened, much less understand why Manuela felt so discouraged after the interaction.

Let's look at how Authentic Dialogue helped Manuela have a conversation with Dr. Jones. Authentic Dialogue is rooted in Nonviolent Communication. It uses and expands on the building blocks of Nonviolent Communication to provide a framework that makes it more likely our attempts to reconnect will lead to increased mutual understanding, rather than more disconnection. We start with Manuela's first step, an internal exploration of the questions we asked in the previous chapter.

Internal Check

Manuela spent several hours deciding whether to speak to Dr. Jones about the differences she perceived in the interactions Dr. Jones had with Manuela and with Lara. As she reflected on the experience, she began to question herself. Maybe she was making a big deal out of nothing? So what, if Dr. Jones seemed much warmer to Lara and other white students than she had been to Manuela? People don't control who they vibe with, and maybe there was something Manuela was doing that didn't invite the same openness as the other students. But as Manuela reflected, she realized she was falling into a pattern that many people who experience microaggressions face. It's always easy to come up with alternate, logical reasons for the actions that might even be true. But regardless of why Dr. Jones responded the way she did to Manuela and Lara, the difference had been painful for Manuela.

It is impossible to determine if unconscious bias was a factor in why Dr. Jones responded so differently to Lara. That gray area—not knowing why someone treats you differently—is one of the challenges many Global Majority people face. Repeatedly dealing with that uncertainty has an impact—people can develop beliefs that either something is flawed with them or the world around them is not accepting. Manuela decided she wanted to talk with Dr. Jones as one way of affirming that the impact Manuela experienced mattered, regardless of Dr. Jones's intention. Before asking Dr. Jones to meet, Manuela began by answering each of the three questions we identified in Chapter 5. Doing so helped Manuela clarify her intentions and whether a dialogue with Dr. Jones was indeed the next step.

Am I Truly Seeking Dialogue?

As Manuela reflected on this question, she realized she was nervous about exploring with Dr. Jones what led to the differences in how Dr. Jones responded to Manuela and how she responded to Lara. Dr. Jones is a well-known person in their field, and Manuela worried about the consequences of speaking up if Dr. Jones were to take offense. Manuela recalled that she had valued receiving Dr. Jones's expertise and guidance in the past and realized she was open to hearing whatever might emerge from their dialogue. As Manuela weighed both the worry and her past appreciation of Dr. Jones, she determined that she wanted to share her experience since it is one that happens in other professional settings, to her and to other Global Majority people.

Why Is This Dialogue Important to Me?

Manuela was clear that this dialogue came at a point in her career where she felt ready to address ways that unconscious bias might impact the experiences of professionals like herself. When she considered the possibility that Dr. Jones's response was the result of unconscious bias, Manuela was motivated to have the dialogue. She wanted to be part of the conversations that are necessary for change to happen that will enable everyone, regardless of their background, to get support and encouragement. Manuela also considered the possibility that there was something about how she presented herself as an individual that stimulated Dr. Jones's reaction. Manuela was open to hearing that and learning from it, although for her this seemed a less likely possibility.

What Am I Seeking from the Other Person?

Manuela was not fully clear about what she wanted. She wanted Dr. Jones to hear her nondefensively but understood that she cannot control how Dr. Jones responds. Manuela realized that what she wanted was for Dr. Jones to be willing to listen to her, to reflect her understanding of Manuela's words, and to share as openly as possible her experience of the situation. Manuela realized she valued brainstorming some possible next steps, regardless of what emerged as the reason for the difference in Dr. Jones's responses to Lara and Manuela.

As Manuela completed this internal check, she became clear that although she was upset about the differential treatment, at this point she was curious about what was going on and hopeful about identifying strategies to reduce the likelihood of it happening again. Despite her worries about the potential cost of speaking up, when Manuela connected to her passion around advocating for more inclusive, welcoming environments for Global Majority professionals, she felt motivated to engage in a conversation. Manuela approached Dr. Jones and invited her to a dialogue.

The Ask

When inviting someone to dialogue, it's helpful to clearly state why you want to meet with them, what you're hoping to explore, and what your desired outcome is. This prevents the person from being caught off guard and gives them an opportunity to do any work they might need to do (e.g., refresh their memory on what happened, get support if they are upset) before having the conversation and to figure out if they need any support during the conversation. Whatever you say here is not fixed and immutable. You're stating your intentions at the start, with full awareness that information emerging during the conversation may shift your understanding of the situation and your intention. Here is Manuela's ask:

Hi, Dr. Jones. I appreciated the chance to talk with you earlier today. I left the conversation feeling confused and disturbed about how it unfolded. I'd like to share my experience and my concern about how unconscious bias might have shown up in our interaction, and I'd like to understand your experience as well. My hope is that the conversation will help us understand each other and create a welcoming atmosphere for all students. Is there some time today or tomorrow that might work for us to meet?

The Dialogue

Authentic Dialogue is a dance in which each party involved has an opportunity to express their truth and get some sense that it was received. Nonviolent Communication provides some structures that can increase the likelihood that what's important to us is received and understood, not defensively blocked, by the folks we are engaging with. When we engage in Authentic Dialogue, we aim to include the four components of the Nonviolent Communication process—observations, feelings, needs, and requests—in our expression. We'll model these components in the dialogue below, then discuss them. As you read the dialogue, you'll notice it focuses on Manuela applying the Authentic Dialogue framework that you will see laid out in Chapter 7.

This is the conversation in which Manuela, the Receiver, shared her experience with Dr. Jones. Dr. Jones, the Actor, is a well-meaning person who is very committed to antiracist practices but may not be aware of how unconscious bias might manifest in her own interactions with Global Majority people. It is most often the case that only one person in a conversation is applying the concepts of Authentic Dialogue, as Manuela is doing here. This person is most often the Receiver or a Bystander, but it is also possible for the Actor to follow these steps, as you will see in later chapters.

Authentic Dialogue: Manuela Molina and Dr. Jones

MANUELA MOLINA: Thank you, Dr. Jones, for agreeing to meet with me. I wanted to talk with you about my experience of our conversation earlier today. I noticed that when you were speaking with me, there were a lot of pauses and silences and that I was just about always the person to initiate breaking those silences. I didn't see you ask me any questions about myself or even elaborate whenever I asked you a question. When you responded, you generally gave one response and then nothing else. When Lara came over, however, I saw a completely different interaction between the two of you. You asked her about where she was from and about her work and then shared at length about your work. I want to first stop and check to see if you have a sense that this is matching what you experienced during that conversation?

DR. JONES: Well, thank you for bringing this to me. As you are sharing, I know we had a conversation with me, you, and Lara, but I'm not remembering it that way. I thought we had a lovely chat. I remember we were chatting and then Lara joined us. I just really enjoyed my time with you all.

MANUELA MOLINA: Okay, it's helpful for me to hear that you didn't notice a huge difference in the conversations. So I'm wondering if you could just hear what I want to share and agree that this was my experience of the conversation. That these are the things I noticed, and they were different from what you saw. There's a bit more I want to add about my experience. Would that work?

DR. JONES: Yeah, yeah.

MANUELA MOLINA: Okay. So what was really hard for me about that interaction was that it brought up a lot of the challenges I and some of my friends of color experience repeatedly. The interactions we have with mentors and professionals often seem to be really different than our white colleagues' interactions. We don't get the same kind of welcome or the same curiosity about who we are. There also seems to be a lack of awareness when it's happening. It's part of what I'm hearing you say today. We're experiencing the difference and, like today, I had very clear indicators of what was different, but it doesn't seem to land that way for you. I feel disheartened experiencing this over and over again, because I worry that it's an example of the kind of unconscious bias experienced by people of color, that doesn't get named and doesn't get addressed. I want everybody to have full access to the mentoring and support they need for their work. Instead, I feel hopeless when I see how these behaviors affect our experience in the workplace.

DR. JONES: Yeah. Yeah, I guess I first just want to say I think you're a lovely person. You know, I love to see that you were part of this program, and it was great to connect with you. And that I do care that everybody in our programs feels valued.

MANUELA MOLINA: I want to interrupt because I'm trusting that so much. Part of the reason I was able to bring this up was that I've heard you speak about how much you value inclusion and that you've done things like supported scholarships and helped people get into the programs. Without my trust in your intentions and interest, I don't think I would have the courage to bring it up. And the piece that I'm wanting to name though is that for so many people, it's not enough to get into these programs and to get into these spaces. I see people leaving after they get in because they are not met with the same kind of welcome and encouragement and interest. And that's part of why I'm bringing it to you, because I think that if more people become aware about this and track it, we could start to shift to a culture where everyone knows they are valued and can really thrive.

DR. JONES: Yeah, I'm hearing that this level of welcoming is really important for you and that it didn't happen for you in our interaction today.

MANUELA MOLINA: I'm appreciating just hearing that you get that this was my experience, and why it matters. I worry that it's more common than you realize and might explain why some people of color don't succeed even when they're invited into these programs. I really want to see if we share an understanding about this dynamic. I think it would help me settle if I got a sense of what comes up for you when you hear me talk about this.

DR. JONES: Yeah. What comes up for me as the head of this program is that we have had so many discussions and there is so much intentionality behind our program. And what I'm hearing right now is that even in this interaction that you and I had outside of program space, at a social event, there is still more work to do to create change. And I'm just struck with how I showed up. I want to make sense of that.

MANUELA MOLINA: I feel such relief hearing you say that. I get you trust I see the intentionality you all are bringing in designing this program. And that you see, "Wow, this was a place we weren't aware of where we can create change and where we can have an impact on people's experiences." I have some ideas around how we could start to tackle this. It might involve actively checking in with other participants of color from the past five years. You can ask what their experience was around this issue of intangible factors that affect whether or not they feel welcome or that they belong here, and what they would like to see happen to address that. If you get a sense that this truly is a problem, I'd love to see the faculty brainstorm how to deal with it, based on what you heard the participants want. Then you can check in with them to see if what you came up with might actually help. Is this something you'd be willing to do?

DR. JONES: Yes, yes, I think we can all benefit from that.

MANUELA MOLINA: Okay, thank you. I feel so strongly about how important this is. Can I check in with you in three months to hear what you're finding out?

DR. JONES: Yes. That timeframe should work for us to begin touching base with other students. I'll know then if we need to do a more extensive review of the issue in the program.

MANUELA MOLINA: Great. I don't think I'm ready to do it now, but I'd love a chance at another time to talk to you about some of the things I'm interested in and to hear more about your work. But right now, I'm just grateful for this conversation. Thank you.

Unpacking the Dialogue

Observations

Let's unpack this dialogue. Manuela began the conversation with the first component of the Nonviolent Communication process—observations. She described the external observations and then checked to see if she and Dr. Jones shared the same understanding of what happened. Many antiracist conversations often start where people haven't actually had a shared experience. This is part of what makes them so immensely challenging to navigate. Since cognitive biases can impact what we notice or remember, don't get into an argument about whether something happened. As Manuela did in this conversation, we can acknowledge that there is a difference in perception and ask to be heard about our experience.

Manuela offered a systemic observation when she referenced an experience of many Global Majority people—that they experience less mentorship and allyship at work. Although Manuela could have offered research documenting this lack of mentorship, it's important to note that she should not feel compelled to offer proof in order for her impression of dynamics that are impacting her to be acknowledged.[1] To make one more systemic observation, often in such instances the burden of the work falls on the Receiver, many times a Global Majority person, who is regularly asked by the Actor, often a white person, to produce the research that backs up their experience.

When we discuss systemic observations related to racism, we are referring to patterns of behaviors in our communities, patterns that one group may experience or be aware of more than another group. This is one of the tips you can take from this discussion. If you are a white person in a situation where, as is often the case, you have had a different experience of an interaction and don't have the knowledge about the systemic context for the Global Majority person who is bringing up the issue, don't privilege only experience that is backed up with data. This is another strategy that serves to support white supremacy culture, even if this is the last thing you would want.

Many things that are commonly known by Receivers of systemic racism have existed and had an impact long before those with the money, education, and power to do so decided to research and document systemic racism in ways that the larger society would accept as valid. An example is the overpolicing of Black and Brown communities. All those who insisted that overpolicing was not happening before research proved otherwise were denying the experiences that so many folks tried to point out. If someone shares their experience that something is widespread, stay curious about their experience and the experience of others. Do so not from the stance of having them produce cases to back up their experience, but rather, from a desire to understand what they are perceiving and what feelings and needs might have been stimulated as a result.

Feelings

Knowing our feelings in response to a stimulus provides an entryway into understanding our needs. Sometimes we are aware of our needs immediately. More often, we are aware only of a physical or emotional response. Manuela, who has been doing this work for some time, might use the awareness of her physical sensations to connect to her emotions and then to her needs. I imagine that Manuela began to notice tightness in her shoulders and a sinking feeling in her stomach while talking with Dr. Jones at the social gathering. After leaving that conversation, Manuela might reflect on those sensations and realize: "My shoulders are still so tight. My stomach is upset." Noticing these sensations could stimulate curiosity: "Am I feeling angry? Am I feeling lonely?" When we identify and witness what is true for us, we often begin to ground. Manuela might notice the tightness begin to ease and her stomach begin to settle. She could continue to deepen her connection to her feelings by asking, "When I connect to loneliness and anger, do other feelings arise? Ahh, am I noticing a deep grief? Am I feeling despair?"

Once we understand our feelings, we can use them to help us connect to what is important to us. An important tenet of Nonviolent Communication is an understanding that our feelings arise from our experience of whether our needs are met or unmet. When we experience a need as met, we might experience a set of feelings that are often labeled as positive (e.g., happy, delighted, satisfied, eager, hopeful). When we experience a need as unmet, we might experience a set of feelings that are often labeled as negative (e.g., frustrated, sad, hopeless, angry, exhausted). Each of us has our own individual map connecting our feelings and needs that is formed by our individual personality, familial patterns, and cultural conditioning.

For example, children all over the world engage in activities that allow them to meet their needs for competence and growth. Many children are excited and proud when they succeed: "Mommy, look! I'm really good at riding a bike now!" Some families will hear a child expressing this and respond with warmth and encouragement: "Ooh, I'm so happy when I see how proud you are that you didn't give up and now you can zoom around so fast on that bike!" Other families might respond with correction and shaming: "It's rude to boast. You're just going to make yourself look silly. After all, you're still wobbly every time you turn." The child in the first family who receives acceptance and warmth might develop a mental map that connects mastery to feelings of delight and satisfaction. The child in the second family who is criticized might develop a different mental map that connects mastery to a complicated stew of satisfaction, fear, and loneliness. Each person can reflect on what emotions they experience when different needs are met to understand their relationship with those needs. Understanding this helps us to hold curiosity and compassion when someone has a different emotional reaction in a situation than we might expect (see the Appendix, Figure 6, for a selection of feelings).

Once Manuela understands the layers of her feelings, she

can explore the needs connected to those feelings. She might search her own mental map and realize: "Ahh, I'm feeling loneliness and grief because receiving support and knowing that I'm valued are deeply important to me. And yes, I feel anger and despair because I want everyone, regardless of their group membership, to experience deep acceptance and care." By noticing her feelings and following their connections to her needs, Manuela is able to understand why Dr. Jones's actions were so distressing to her. Each person may have a different set of feelings and needs stimulated by the same situation. When Manuela attempted to talk to Lara, her friend who joined the conversation with Dr. Jones, she discovered Lara had a different experience. Lara's need for support and care had been met, and Lara reported feeling satisfied and excited about the conversation. Although Lara was aware that Dr. Jones was speaking more to her than to Manuela, Lara assumed this was a onetime experience limited to this interaction and did not share the same systemic observations that Manuela did.

You may have noticed that in the dialogue with Dr. Jones, Manuela reported she felt "disheartened" instead of using the actual feelings—despair and grief—which she had identified in her self-exploration before the dialogue. Sharing our feelings with another is a deeply vulnerable act. Many folks, especially Global Majority people, have experienced that when sharing feelings, we are told they are "too big," "wrong," or otherwise problematic. In work settings many folks, especially Global Majority people, learn that some feelings are considered inappropriate, "too much," or unprofessional.

It's important to assess the level of risk we are willing and able to take on when we engage in dialogue. Manuela assumed a significant degree of risk in bringing this issue to Dr. Jones who, because she is a senior in their field, has the power to impact Manuela's professional opportunities. While Manuela was willing to share her experience with Dr. Jones, she worried that expressing the depth of her feelings—naming the despair, anger, and hopelessness she felt—could result in her being dismissed as overly dramatic and being stereotyped as the angry Latina. One might argue whether or not Manuela should give any weight to these concerns. I believe that in an ideal world, when we can bring our full authentic selves to our dialogues, we create the greatest opportunities for change. This is what the legions of committed nonviolent activists have done—they spoke up fearlessly and courageously, at tremendous risk to themselves, to have their experience fully known. The assessment of how much we are willing to risk in a dialogue is discussed more fully below.

Needs

As we move through the world, we are motivated to attend to what we value, the things that are important to us. Nonviolent Communication rests on the premise that regardless of race, ethnicity, place of origin, or other forms of identity, humans all share the same set of needs. These can broadly be grouped into physical needs, freedom, connection, and meaning. This universality represents qualities that transcend any specific individual preference or strategy, worldview, or group and cultural norms. In the conversation Manuela shared several needs that motivated her desire for dialogue—for everyone to know they are valued, supported in their work, and have a shared understanding. Sharing the needs we are aware of that are relevant to our situation is an essential aspect of

Authentic Dialogue. When Manuela shared her needs, separate from her strategies, Dr. Jones was more likely to hear what was important to Manuela and understand why it was important.

If we share only our strategies—in this case, "I wanted you to ask me questions about me and share more freely about your work"—it is easier for people to challenge the specific strategy. Dr. Jones, hearing only a strategy, could wonder: "Why do you want me to ask you questions? Why don't you ask me questions? If you want to learn about my work, why don't you read my website?" If Dr. Jones hears the need for being valued and for support behind the strategy, it's more difficult to dismiss its importance. Dr. Jones might question why Manuela believes a specific strategy is helpful but is more likely to understand the need itself. Speaking about our needs, or listening for the needs when someone is speaking to us, can create a bridge for understanding someone's behavior with more compassion (see the Appendix, Figure 7, for a sample list of needs).

We all have different strategies to attend to our needs, and those strategies might change over time. It's easy to assume our preferred strategy is universally preferred. Manuela's request that Dr. Jones check with the students about their needs is based on this seemingly obvious truism. Without asking the Global Majority people about their needs and their preferred strategies, it would be easy for Dr. Jones to assume her needs in the situation were also theirs, and that what would work for Dr. Jones would also work for them. This unconscious centering of the needs and strategies of white people when there is a conflict is another way that white supremacy culture manifests.

Requests

We have explored the importance of knowing your intentions and the specific needs you hope to meet when seeking dialogue. Manuela's intention in speaking with Dr. Jones was to contribute to a shift in the experience that Global Majority people have in professional settings. After sharing with Dr. Jones her observations, feelings, and needs, Manuela followed up with requests—the steps she asked Dr. Jones to take. Requests are the catalyst that fires the engine of possibility and moves us along the path from awareness of the present reality to the future we envision. Without requests, of ourselves or of other people, nothing changes. We might become aware of what is not working for us but not have the mechanism to transform it into something that serves us better. If we share our needs without making requests, the other person must guess what is important to us and choose how to act differently. It is highly probable that the person may choose a strategy that does not create the change that we seek. Requests are the mechanism for a more satisfactory change.

Making a request is deeply vulnerable. To make a request means we are stating to ourselves that our needs matter and that they can also matter to the other person. Many of us do not firmly trust that our experiences and our needs do matter, especially if we frequently experience rejection and denials when making requests. This experience can be even more pronounced for those impacted by white supremacy culture, where white people's needs are prioritized at the expense and even denial of the needs of Global Majority people. The vulnerability required to make a request will increase in proportion to our lack of trust in our mattering. Without that trust, it can be unbearably vulnerable and risky to make a request and open ourselves up to someone who may have already demonstrated that they may not be holding our needs with care.

Many of us are conditioned to experience a negative response to our request as rejection of us, or as confirmation that what is important to us is indeed not important to others. We can begin to shift that belief by recognizing that when people say no to our requests, it is not necessarily a no to us but rather may be that person's attempt to say yes to their own needs. Sometimes people may be aware enough to explicitly say: "I wish I could, but I need to…." When we hear that, we often relax. But sometimes the person may not have the awareness of why they are saying no. Develop a practice of asking yourself "What are they saying yes to?" This allows you to counter the story you may have internalized that can make it so hard to risk asking for what will meet your needs.

Practitioners of Nonviolent Communication often delineate two types of requests I find helpful to track in Authentic Dialogue: solution requests and connection requests. Solution requests attend to the content that drives the dialogue—what we need to do to address the needs we've identified. Connection requests attend to the process of the dialogue—what we need to do to move to the level of connection necessary to work out a solution that addresses the needs we have identified without it being at a cost to the other person.[2] As Manuela and Dr. Jones spoke, Manuela made several connection requests. First, she checked in about Dr. Jones's willingness to talk with her. Then, after sharing her initial observations, Manuela asked to hear if those experiences were shared by Dr. Jones. Later in the dialogue, Manuela asked Dr. Jones to share her reaction to Manuela's expression. Connection requests like these provide opportunities to check in on some of the variables that impact the relationship. These requests can serve to establish some trust in our intention to hold each other with care.

Solution requests center around the actions one might take to address the challenges that were identified. Manuela asked Dr. Jones to hear from other Global Majority participants, to increase the faculty and staff's awareness of the challenges around inclusion. She asked that the faculty commit to working on solutions that incorporate participants' desires and that they confirm with Global Majority participants that the solutions that the faculty identify seem potentially helpful. Solution requests ideally should focus on specific actions that are doable. Ask yourself: "What need am I trying to meet? What can I or another person do that is likely to meet that need? How will I know when this need has been met?" Avoid nonspecific requests or statements of what we don't want. For example, Manuela might attempt to make a request by saying to Dr. Jones: "I don't want you to ignore Global Majority people during group conversations." Dr. Jones might say yes and then, in the absence of clear actionable requests from Manuela, attempt to identify what would be satisfying for Manuela. She might make a concerted effort to smile and make eye contact with Global Majority people in her groups. She might start each group by going to Global Majority participants and introducing herself. As she does this, she feels satisfied that she has met Manuela's request. If we want our requests to be powerful, we need to take the risk and ask for *exactly* what we do want.

A daring request Manuela might make could be: "I'd like you to gain the capacity to truly engage with people of color in your workshops. Can you record the next few workshops, and quantify how much time you spend talking to white people and to people of color, and what kinds of questions you ask the white people that you don't ask people of color? Then I'd like you to hold an intention to ask similar questions of people of color at the same rate you asked white people, recording yourself and checking if you do. Can you commit to trying this strategy?" The specificity of the request would contribute to Manuela's trust that if Dr. Jones says yes, it might lead to the change that they are both looking for. And if Dr. Jones says no, it will be easier for Manuela to guess the needs Dr. Jones might be attempting to meet by saying no. They could then work together to find a different strategy that attends to both their needs. When we don't ask for what we want, we can end up dissatisfied with the outcome even when someone has said yes to us.

We may gain more personal and collective power when we take the risk to identify what's important to us and to others, and work together to find strategies that might work for all. But we also need to acknowledge that some people may have less spaciousness about crafting requests that attend to everyone's needs. For example, people from groups who have suffered the impact of white supremacy beliefs and who have watched their needs go unmet, individually and collectively, for generations may not have the energy or desire to include the needs of members of the dominant group (the person/people with the most amount of structural or relational power and privilege in the situation) in their requests. Indeed, it can be seen as an act of protest not to do so. A white supremacy belief that is often functioning without anyone's conscious awareness is that the needs of white people must be prioritized and attended to at all times. In this case it may be necessary to act against this belief. We can do so by neither prioritizing nor excluding the needs of white people when searching for new strategies.

As we work toward building Beloved Community, I believe we can hold an intention to move away from the either/or binary of whose needs are being cared for, to envision a world where everyone can be supported at the same time. And if someone does not have the capacity to stretch into that vision, I don't want to insist that they do. Instead, I can hold that commitment and take on the extra work to envision and check what their needs are, and to bring mine into the mix. As people experience that their needs are being attended to more and more, they will increase their capacity to hold more than just their own needs. In Chapter 7 we will learn the Authentic Dialogue framework, a tool that supports conversations aimed at helping us surface everyone's needs and create the connection necessary to find strategies to better address them all.

NOTES

1. Bryan Hancock, James Manyika, Monne Williams, and Lareina Yee, "The Black Experience at Work in Charts," *McKinsey Quarterly* (December 13, 2021), https://www.mckinsey.com/featured-insights /diversity-and-inclusion/the-black-experience-at-work-in-charts.

2. Inbal Kashtan and Miki Kashtan, "Connection Requests: Motivations and Examples," in *2014 BayNVC Nonviolent Communication Leadership Program* (Oakland, CA: BayNVC, 2014), 31–34.

7

The Authentic Dialogue Framework

In previous chapters I have introduced the various concepts and practices that form the Authentic Dialogue framework. This chapter lays out the complete framework and reviews each component.

The Components of the Authentic Dialogue Framework

Consciousness

Authentic Dialogue is grounded in a firm commitment to several principles (Figure 5). First, we hold the creation of Beloved Community, in which everyone is valued and we work together so everyone can thrive, as our ultimate goal. Even if we are unlikely to live in a time when the systems and structures around us reflect the values of Beloved Community, we aim *now* to operate in the world, as much as possible, in ways that do. This commitment means that when a member of our community says or does something that is painful for us to experience, we strive to connect to their humanity, to see them as a welcomed community member and not someone we must oust.

The second principle of Authentic Dialogue supports us in connecting to the other's humanity by reminding us that human beings are always attempting to meet needs, needs that we all have, in everything they do or say. When someone does something we don't like, even something with significant impact on us or on what we deeply care for, we can connect to their humanity by trying to understand the very human needs they are attempting to meet, even as we let them know the actions they are taking are too costly to us. This stance invites us to hold the possibility that a person is not irreparably evil. Indeed, people who say or do things that are harmful, such as many actions emerging from white supremacy ideas or other oppressive beliefs, benefit from community intervention to stop them from committing further harm. This intervention can also guide them toward different actions that can better meet their and the community's needs. No one, including those folks who say and do things that are harmful, is discarded.

The third principle of the Authentic Dialogue framework acknowledges that white supremacy beliefs and other ideologies have led to and continue to result in systemic oppression of certain groups. These ideologies impact the ways in which people experience the world—what they pay attention to and, because of cognitive biases, what they are even able to perceive. White supremacy culture may also impact the range of strategies people deem acceptable to meet their needs. Acknowledging the existence of white supremacy thinking and other oppressive ideologies invites us to see the individual

Authentic Dialogue Framework

Preparation

Consciousness:

- Affirm the commitment to Beloved Community as the ultimate goal guiding each step of this dialogue.
- Remember all human behavior is motivated by needs.
- Acknowledge the existence of white supremacy thinking and other forms of oppression.
- Aim for solutions that advance our collective liberation.

Inner Work:

- Clarify what happened. What is the external observation?
- Surface any thoughts or judgments.
- Ask what might have been missed? Are cognitive biases impacting perception?
- Identify the internal observation. What memories and experiences were triggered?
- Determine what systemic observations were stimulated.
- Scan your body and identify sensations and emotions.
- Self-empathize to gain clarity on needs.
- Identify your purpose in asking for a dialogue.
- Determine what risk you are willing to accept balancing your needs and your intention to move toward Beloved Community.
- Identify barriers to dialogue.

Core Dialogue

Dialogue **to Be Heard**

- Use connection requests in every element of the dialogue.
- Make the ask: Check willingness for dialogue.
- Make agreements to attend to any barriers that exist.
- Determine together if everyone will be heard. If more than one person will share, determine who shares first.
- Listening Steps:
    - Reflect the person's experience.
    - Empathize with all levels of impact.
    - Acknowledge systemic contributions.

Expanded Dialogues

Dialogue for
Healing

- Begin with a ***Dialogue to Be Heard.***
- Give space for Receiver to connect with and express emotional impact and be received with deep empathy.
- Identify any meaning and unconscious contracts that the Receiver holds in relation to the act.
- If Receiver is willing, consider possible needs motivating the Actor's action.
- Mourn unmet needs.
- Ensure that each participant seeking healing is the focus of the listening steps.
- If clarity emerges that an action is desired, move to Dialogue for Solution.

Dialogue for
Shared Understanding

- Begin with a ***Dialogue to Be Heard***.
- Mourn unmet needs.
- Ensure each participant has an opportunity to express their experience and receive empathy.
- If clarity emerges that an action is desired, move to Dialogue for Solution.

Dialogue for
Solution

- Begin with a ***Dialogue to Be Heard.***
- Ensure each impacted person has an opportunity to express their needs.
- Summarize all needs identified.
- Brainstorm strategies to attend to as many needs as possible.
- Generate solution requests.
- Select solution prioritizing, attending to as many needs as possible, including needs around equity.
- Agree on implementation timeline.
- Make agreements about follow-up.

FIGURE 5. Authentic Dialogue © Mireille van Bremen and Roxy Manning

acting from these beliefs not as an enemy, but as someone also adversely impacted by these ideologies who will need support to see how these beliefs are not in the service of Beloved Community. We can hold boundaries and enact policies to prevent ongoing harm and to counter the effect of these ideologies, creating space while the multifaceted, challenging work of system change continues.

This leads into the fourth aspect of Authentic Dialogue consciousness—looking for solutions in support of our well-being and our collective liberation. In order to work toward Beloved Community, we search for inclusive solutions—ones that do not leave anyone behind. I cannot be truly liberated if any person is oppressed. This is in direct opposition to a central practice that emerges from white supremacy beliefs. We reject the *prioritization, no matter the cost,* of the needs of white people. Indeed, the idea that any group should be prioritized a priori over other groups is untenable. Instead, we work to understand everyone's needs, Global Majority *and* white, and hold them all equally important. As we search for solutions that truly allow all groups to thrive, we enhance our capacity to undo the effects and eliminate causes of social oppression.[1]

Inner Work

As you can see, Authentic Dialogue starts before we actually engage in conversation with other people. In addition to reaffirming the elements of the consciousness of Authentic Dialogue, we take steps to do the internal work that makes it more likely that what we say and the strategies that we advance will be in alignment with that consciousness. The inner work of Authentic Dialogue includes gaining clarity on what we are experiencing, understanding which values we are aiming to meet in the moment, determining our purpose in asking for dialogue, assessing the degree of risk we can assume, and identifying and attending to any barriers to an effective dialogue.

Begin the inner work by clarifying your understanding of what happened. What was the external observation? Notice your thoughts and judgments. What are you telling yourself about the other person or the situation? What stories do you have about who they are, what they stand for, what that signifies? Are they good/bad, are you safe/unsafe, and so on? These judgments can get in the way of us seeing the person and situation fully and reduce the likelihood that we will see them as part of our Beloved Community. Instead, question these stories and judgments. Are there cognitive biases impacting what you perceive and what you pay attention to? Notice those biases and ask what other information you might be missing because of them. What would be a more complete picture of what is happening? Continue to acknowledge other observations that might be present. What memories or prior experiences did the event stimulate? What systemic patterns or impacts are now in your awareness, triggered by the external observation?

As you connect to your observations, notice how they are affecting and impacting your physical body. Scan your body for any sensations and emotions that arise in response to these observations. They provide crucial information that can help you understand what you value. As you notice each sensation and emotion, ask yourself: "What need or value do I have that is stimulating this emotion right now? Am I having this reaction in response to that need or value being met or not met? What is important to me in this moment?" People often have different responses to the same situation. Being clear on what you value is an essential aspect of Authentic Dialogues. This clarity will inform the next steps of the inner work as well as the actual dialogue.

Once we have more clarity on what happened, what is important to us and our emotions in relation to the event, we are ready for the next step. From this place of self-understanding, ask yourself: *What am I seeking from the other person? What is my purpose in requesting a dialogue?* We might be looking to be heard about our experience, to experience a sense of healing, to support an understanding of what happened that encompasses multiple perspectives, and/or to find a solution that addresses what happened. Getting clear on what we need and what we hope the dialogue will accomplish increases the possibility, should the dialogue happen, of attending to the needs that we have. This combination—clarity of observation, deep understanding of self, clarity of needs, and clarity of purpose—allows us to take the caring and fiercely real stance that is the goal of Authentic Dialogue. Knowing what our purpose is allows us to choose our path through Authentic Dialogue.

On Choosing to Risk and Not to Risk

Once we are clear what we want to have an Authentic Dialogue about and which path we will follow, we need to look at what we're willing to risk in having this dialogue. Here is one of the dilemmas of Authentic Dialogue. I am asking us to risk showing up, with our full, vulnerable truth, committed to engaging with another person as a step toward Beloved Community. I'm asking us to do so, even when we don't know if the other person shares our values. Why would we take this risk? Because our whole intention is to take action that brings us closer to Beloved Community. Risking is a step toward trusting that our needs matter. Even if the other person refuses to acknowledge us, it's a step that says that *we* refuse to buy into a belief that our needs are unimportant, don't matter, don't exist. Instead, each time we risk, we take a step closer to trusting that we and others believe something different. We affirm: "We're here. We matter. Our needs matter."

Before choosing to go into dialogue, we reflect on what individually we *are* willing to risk. What are the possible costs of speaking up? What needs would we meet by choosing to risk in this moment? Holding both our fierce commitment to Beloved Community and our care for ourselves and our well-being, we invite clear intention and choice about entering the dialogue and how far to go. And we hold each decision on what to risk and how much to risk without judgment. Beloved Community encompasses those who choose options along the entire spectrum. It includes those making the difficult choice to risk everything, even their lives, to radically shift our systems. It also acknowledges and includes those choosing the hard task of not risking in order to care for children, elders, the functioning of the community or to safeguard their emotional well-being. We choose dialogue, deciding how much or little to risk, knowing that each time we try, we add a stone—some giant pavers and some small pebbles—on the path toward Beloved Community.

My colleague Edmundo Norte speaks of the possibilities that vulnerably risking can spark to support our social justice work. When we take a chance to model a more authentic, vulnerable way of being, he notes, we may awaken a shared understanding of what is possible in those who witness us, possibly inspiring them to join us in this new way of being. As more people contemplate—and risk—trying out this previously unimagined possibility, we seed together the beginning of social change.

At the same time, there are very real reasons why we might choose *not* to risk sharing our full truth, *not* to continue speaking in the face of resistance, or even *not* to speak at all. The impact of generations of practices and systems grounded in white supremacy beliefs means that many Global Majority people are vulnerable in many ways—economically, physically, socially, and so on. We've watched community members be murdered for speaking authentically and resisting injustice. Some of us might need to keep a job or finish that last class and get the degree we've been working on. Some of us are worried there will be repercussions from people who see our speaking up as the cause of their job loss or loss of access to things that they value. We may choose not to risk for intangible reasons as well. We may worry about losing a friendship or losing hope. There are myriad reasons why we might choose not to risk.

I want to be clear that the invitation to risk is not only for Global Majority people. White people *must show up* and be willing to step out of the safe shelter that whiteness and the lack of direct impact can afford them. Global Majority people did not create these oppressive systems and do not benefit from them; it is not their responsibility alone to dismantle them. When I speak to white people about this work, many realize that even when they know how to speak up, they can (and sadly too often) choose not to, unconsciously prioritizing their comfort, desire for competency, and need for safety.

Global Majority people often don't get that choice, especially in situations when they are being explicitly singled out for harm. For white people, in addition to all the reasons described earlier, risking is a form of solidarity.

I want to acknowledge that Global Majority people have been collectively risking for change to happen. We are stronger as a group, and as a group we can continue to work to mitigate the risk of our individual members. When we see ourselves as a group working for liberation together, any individual can step back when they are exhausted. If anyone is harmed from risking, we can step in to stop further harm and heal them. We can choose not to risk in moments when the potential harm is more than we accept. Each of us is a drop in the river of resistance, relentlessly wearing down the bank of white supremacy culture. Individually our impact might vary, we might not even touch the bank as we move by. But collectively, united, we build momentum—whether we're touching the bank or adding to the momentum of the stream—and are unstoppable.

Barriers

Before beginning the actual Authentic Dialogue, the last piece of the inner work is identifying what might get in the way of having the dialogue. Think about this as figuring out what you can address or put in place that would make it more likely you and the other person will both show up fully and authentically for the dialogue. There are a number of factors that you might consider. Some basic ones are whether each person is resourced enough to engage in dialogue. Resources can include things that support physical well-being such as having enough rest and access to food. It includes attending to the location. Is there sufficient privacy so that each person has a sense of choice about the amount of disclosure and possible risk they are taking? Is the location sufficiently neutral? Scheduling a discussion about police brutality in a police station might not afford all the participants an equitable sense of familiarity and safety, for example.

You also want to consider barriers to emotional participation. Those involved in the dialogue may have habits of domination and submission, learned through their interpersonal relationships and how society relates to them based on their group identity, that could lead them to adopt white supremacy culture beliefs. A Black client once told me she wouldn't even attempt to be authentic with her white male supervisor because in past attempts he spoke over her, contradicted her, and used most of any agreed-upon meeting time to clarify *his* position. After participating in several such dialogues, she gave up and now sits quietly through meetings, waiting for them to end. In situations like these, full participation might be supported if a mediator helped to track and support each voice to be fully heard.

There have also been occasions when someone was clear that the level of fear or distress that they were experiencing was such that they needed another person present to provide empathic support or advocacy for them to have enough courage to speak. Conversely, I've had people tell me they wanted an additional presence in the dialogue, because they were no longer willing to offer support to the Actor. They described sharing how they were impacted by something the Actor did, only to have the Actor express deep shame, then turn to them—the Receiver—for emotional support about the Actor's feelings of shame, completely ignoring the content the

Receiver shared. Some of these Receivers were only willing to attempt another dialogue with the Actor if someone else was present to offer brief emotional support to the Actor so the Receiver did not have to do so, while also trying to deal with their own vulnerability and stimulation. Acknowledging that we don't enter dialogues with the same comfort and ease, assessing for these barriers and then identifying the steps that might address them is another important piece of the preparatory work for having these dialogues.

Although these elements are presented in a linear order, you may start with any facet of the inner work. You might first be aware of wanting a dialogue because you want mutual understanding, for instance, then check in to see if there are any thoughts or judgments that might influence how you show up in the dialogue. As you go through the steps, you might notice that as you become aware of your needs, you experience other physical sensations that lead you to new feelings and thoughts and then to a whole new set of needs. Asking yourself "Is there more?" can be helpful to increase the likelihood that you have uncovered the broadest range of factors that might impact how the actual dialogue unfolds.

The Dialogues

The next component of the Authentic Dialogue framework is entering one of the four Dialogues. I use "dialogue" to refer to the general exchange of information with an intent to foster understanding, and "Dialogue" to reference one of the four processes I introduce next. We enter the dialogue phase firmly grounded in our intention that they take place within the larger goal of creating Beloved Community. We begin with our Core Dialogue—Dialogue to Be Heard. Then, guided by our intention, we might move to one of the three remaining dialogues—Dialogue for Healing, Dialogue for Shared Understanding, and Dialogue for Solution.

Dialogue to Be Heard

The Core Dialogue—Dialogue to Be Heard—is our foundational Dialogue and starting point for the other three.

Connection Requests

An underlying principle of the dialogue phase is that tending to the quality of the relationship is as important as focusing on the content of the topic of discussion. Making connection requests is one way that we bring relational acknowledgment into the Dialogue. Doing so holds care for the relationship, increasing the likelihood that regardless of outcome, we are building Beloved Community. We typically begin the Dialogue with a connection request—checking for consent. If we are not certain of the other person's willingness to be in dialogue, we ask. This is one way of demonstrating care for the relationship from the onset. Don't assume authentic willingness is present. Personality differences, habits of compliance, and the multiple ways patterns of oppression intersect and crisscross all might shape someone's ability to consensually engage in dialogue with us. Check the other's willingness, and if it's not there, assess what the person needs to become more willing. Do they need empathy from someone else, do they need a supportive presence, a different time or place, more understanding about the purpose? What else might be helpful?

Connection requests continue throughout the Dialogue.

Connection requests make it possible for us to hold care for the relationship and care for ourselves. For instance, as the Dialogue proceeds, we might ask for a reflection of what we have shared. If the response to that request demonstrates that the listener can hear and reflect back what's important to us, we might relax. As we experience our needs for understanding being met, we might have increased trust and ease in being vulnerable. If the listener is unable to convey what they heard from us, or their reflection is far from how we want to be understood, we might become curious about the barriers to understanding. Perhaps the other is flooded with feelings and needs a moment for self-empathy before they can take in more information. Perhaps they are so resistant to what we're sharing that they are mentally preparing their argument, contesting what we've shared rather than staying present with us.

As we gain information on how we're being received, we can assess our capacity and willingness to continue showing up. Sometimes we might be willing to stretch out of care for the whole, to make it more possible for the listener to hear us in the way we want to be heard. We might choose to invite others to step in to respond to either our or the listener's needs. We might realize that the listener's inability to receive us, or what they are taking away from what we shared, is stimulating our own pain and despair so deeply that we cannot continue in the conversation or might need support from others to do so. Making connection requests throughout the Dialogue enables each person to assess and care for their own well-being, understand how to contribute to the well-being of others in the Dialogue, and tend to the level of trust and understanding between all involved.

Deciding Who Will Be the Focus

As part of establishing the agreement about being in Dialogue, we need to determine who will be the focus of the Dialogue. Whose experience are we attempting to understand? Will everyone participating in the Dialogue share their experience, or is the focus on a specific person sharing their experience, while others who are present reflect and empathize? The person initiating the Dialogue can name what they are inviting listeners into when they make the request.

We can ask for a Dialogue in which we want others to support us with reflection, empathy, or acknowledgment, even as we are clear we are not available to offer the same support to others. Doing so can create spaciousness and focus. While it may seem like a difficult thing to ask for, some people experience relief, especially when they are the Actor, to have a specific idea of how they can show up for these conversations in ways that land as supportive to the Receiver. Knowing that they will offer reflection and empathy but not share their experience, they may find it easier to truly listen. All too often when we have a disagreement with someone, rather than stay fully present while they speak, we use the time when we are in the listening role to prepare what we will say when it's our turn to speak again—to flesh out our arguments, to pick out the inconsistencies in what we're hearing, find the "what about" we can offer as rebuttal. Explicitly agreeing on who will share in each Dialogue to Be Heard or Dialogue for Healing can reduce the need to do this, thus supporting choice and inviting everyone to be intentional.

We can also agree that more than one person will speak. Sometimes we want to hear from everyone who has been impacted. Hearing from everyone may happen over more than one session, sometimes centering just one speaker per session, to care for the ability to maintain focus, especially in the face of intensity. Participants can clarify these options at the beginning, with openness to changing the agreement if the conditions shift.

Deciding Who Speaks First

Once there is agreement for Dialogue and who will be the focus, it's helpful to explicitly decide who speaks first, if relevant. Here, consider prioritizing the needs of the person with the least amount of structural or relational power and privilege in the situation. Allow that person to determine if they wish to share their experience first, or if they would prefer that the other person share first.

Sometimes, because of relational and structural dynamics, those with less rank and power have rarely been heard by people with more power. For some, being the first to share their experience upends a pattern that I have often seen, where the person with more power speaks first for most of the allotted time, leaving very little, if any, room for the person with least structural power to be heard. There can be relief in entering a conversation knowing that there truly will be a chance for you to share. At other times, the person with the least structural power might want the other person to speak first. One colleague acknowledged that when there has been low trust between them and someone with more structural power, they often prefer that the other person speak first. Doing so gives them information on how the person is interpreting what has happened, if they appear open to multiple perspectives or if they are able to apply a systemic lens to the issue. My colleague says this information helps them know if the gap is wide enough between them and the other person that my colleague might need to gather more resources to stay in the conversation with full committment to both authenticity and care.

Listening Steps

The listening steps of the Core Dialogue are rooted in and expand on the consciousness and process of Nonviolent Communication.

Witnessing the Speaker's Experience: We begin by witnessing the experience of the speaker. The speaker shares some aspect of their experience, often beginning with the external observation. Starting with the external observation helps all in the Dialogue tune in to the same act. Even if they don't initially share the same perspective, there is clarity about which perspective is being referenced in the moment. The speaker can share the internal and systemic observations that were stimulated. The speaker's goal in this phase is to show up authentically. Some people worry that they must adopt a certain tone, soften their voice, use specific words to participate in Authentic Dialogue. Not at all!

Instead, we can speak in whatever way is true for us. If we are angry, then our voice might have some intensity, our tone might be sharp. We might speak gently or bluntly. When in the speaker role, we preferably have done the inner work to have clarity about what is important to us and we speak that truth. And we want to stay grounded in the intention that in speaking, we are working toward the possibility of connection, healing, and repair that builds Beloved Community.

Although it is ideal if the speaker has done this work, this is often not the case or even possible. The speaker may be so stimulated that their expression is unfiltered and raw, perhaps without full clarity about which needs were stimulated, what they want back from the listener, or even with judgments and biases unchecked.

Empathy for Speaker: In our role as the listener, we can try to track and support the process of Authentic Dialogue. As listener, regardless of the speaker's manner of expression, we try to acknowledge the impact the speaker experienced. When we acknowledge impact, we aim to understand what needs were not met. The listener empathizes with the speaker, reflecting both the speaker's unmet needs and the emotions that were stimulated as a result. If the speaker is expressing with intensity and judgment, the listener can view that expression as information to help them better understand the breadth and depth of the speaker's experience, rather than demand that the speaker tone it down or say it in a different way before the listener is willing to empathize.

When we empathize with the speaker, we are careful to adopt a stance of curiosity, not certainty. We attempt to connect deeply with the speaker by understanding the relationship between what they experienced or perceived, the needs and values that were important to them in the experience, and how they felt as a result. We check with the speaker to see if our understanding of that relationship and what the speaker valued is resonant with them. It's important to note that the more life experiences and shared belief systems we have with the speaker, the more we share the same perspective, the more ease we might have in connecting to their emotions and their values. Even so, it's still important to check. There are sufficient individual differences between members of the same groups or even within the same family that we don't assume that we correctly understood the speaker's experience.

Acknowledgment of Systemic Issues: An important next step in Authentic Dialogue about systemic issues like racism is that we acknowledge those systemic issues. This acknowledgment often occurs as any systemic observations are shared and empathized with. Receiving this acknowledgment can contribute to a sense of being understood and to healing when the listener is able to demonstrate an awareness of not just the current situation but also how it connects to larger systemic patterns. As we know, the charge we experience in response to an incident can be exacerbated when that incident is one of many that the person or members of their group encounter repeatedly. If the speaker does not connect their specific incident to a larger systemic pattern, but the listener perceives one, the listener can offer to share their perception with the speaker, not as truth but as an exploration. Sometimes the speaker may not want to discuss the possible systemic issue with the listener and will decline the listener's offer.

Try to respect and honor the speaker's limits, as it is not the role of the listener to educate or force their perceptions onto the speaker. Sometimes the speaker welcomes the listener's offer. Some speakers have told me that they have been reluctant to share the systemic awareness they were holding because it had so often been contested or dismissed. When the listener raises the possibility of the systemic issue, the speaker can often experience relief that the topic is not off-limits and that their experience is truly understood.

Both steps—the process of entering the Core Dialogue as well as the content—comprise the foundational Dialogue to Be Heard. As discussed, the process of entering the Dialogue includes checking willingness, determining the speaker, and deciding the order of speakers. The content relates to empathizing with the speaker's experience and acknowledging any systemic factors. Sometimes all we have willingness or capacity for is simply to speak up and to be known for our experience. We can take a stance of empowerment and honoring of our own experience when we no longer silently accept injustice and impacts. Working to make sure others are aware of harm that is happening is a crucial step for social change in the Kingian nonviolence tradition. Some might see this as a form of education.[2]

At an interpersonal level, asking for a Dialogue to Be Heard can serve the function of education of the Actor, though this is not its purpose. People have protested this stance, asserting it's not their job to educate the person who has harmed them. I agree. An Actor can learn about almost any issue and how it manifests in society through countless sources easily available to them. Going to the person impacted by our actions for education places another layer of burden and responsibility onto the person who is already working to hold the impact. Although Dialogues to Be Heard will very likely meet needs for education for the Actor, the primary purpose of this Dialogue is to meet the Receiver's need to be known and to be understood. The Receiver may not be interested in understanding the Actor, or even working on solutions in the moment; expressing and getting reflections back that show that they were understood are enough.

It is my experience that there can be benefit for a Receiver if they are willing to support the Actor's engagement with their privilege. Receivers who do this might experience a greater sense of choice, may grow their capacity to share their experience, and may experience more hope and trust in our shared humanity.

Dialogue for Healing

Sometimes we want a deeper outcome than to have our experience seen and acknowledged. We want healing. Healing can occur on many levels—from shifts in our understanding of events that can help free us from limiting beliefs to tectonic shifts in our relationships with ourselves and the world. A Dialogue for Healing is one of many strategies that can contribute to these kinds of shifts.

As the speaker (likely but not always the Receiver) in a Dialogue for Healing, we are embracing the power of vulnerability. We choose to share the full extent of how we were impacted. We express the full depth of our emotions—anger, despair, grief, fear—emotions that we so often might hide, worried about the cost of exposing them. In sharing these emotions, we invite the listener to enter a field of empathy with us. We ask the listener to be present for the range of our emotions, with nonjudgmental acceptance. We ask the listener to help us unpack the layers of emotions and needs, to help deepen our understanding of what our hearts hold most dear, what we are longing for. We are examining the meaning we are taking from the event. Are we worried that some story about us, or about our group, is being confirmed? Are we taking the event to mean that some people will never be safe? Are we telling ourselves that this event proves that it's too dangerous to try a new behavior, enter a new space, or interact with people outside our group? It can be intensely vulnerable to expose to someone else's gaze the needs that are stimulated or the meaning we make of certain events. In Dialogues for Healing we reveal ourselves in this way, reaching for the relief and changes in perspective that understanding and empathic presence can bring.

As the listener in a Dialogue for Healing (sometimes but not always the Actor), we commit to showing up nonjudgmentally. Our empathic presence is essential here—being able to listen, not just to the observations or judgments a speaker/Receiver shares but also to perceive the feelings and needs underneath. As the speaker/Receiver shares their experience and surfaces the meanings they made from the event, we can reflect back the emotions and needs they may be experiencing in relation to that meaning. We deepen empathy in the Dialogue for Healing, looking at each layer of pain revealed and helping to surface and hold care for the unmet needs. If the speaker/Receiver is willing to consider it, we can offer our understanding of the needs that might have motivated the actions that impacted the Receiver.

When Receivers don't understand why someone took the actions they did, it becomes easier to default to a variation of old stories (e.g., "I'm not safe, that person is dangerous, the world is not safe, everyone is racist, no one sees the true me"). As the listener, when we share a different understanding, rooted in needs, it becomes possible for the speaker/Receiver to consider: "This happened not because I'm bad, or I'm not seen, or they are bad, or the world is horrible, but because this person was trying to attend to their needs and chose a strategy that was devastating to me. There is a possible outcome other than that this will always happen—this person can learn different strategies." We only offer this understanding of the Actor's needs if the speaker/Receiver is open to it. It is very likely that if the speaker/Receiver has not received sufficient empathy for the pain they experienced and the unmet needs that were stimulated, they will not be ready or able to take in an exploration of our needs as the listener/Actor without some sense that their experience is being set aside or discounted.

It is also helpful to mourn the unmet needs. This would involve creating space to fully hear the impact of the stimulus and helping surface the layers of feelings and unmet needs experienced. This is especially true in those Dialogues in which we, as the listener, were the Actor whose choices stimulated pain for the Receiver. As the listener, when we share our mourning, we share the needs we connect to in response to the speaker's expression. As we hear a speaker who is grieving a loss of dignity and care, we may also notice our sorrow as our own deep longing for everyone to experience support, care, and respect is stimulated. Sharing our needs that were stimulated can let the speaker know that their experience has impacted us, that their expression mattered. We still center the speaker/Receiver as we share this—we're not sharing and changing the focus to getting support or even empathy for our awareness of these needs that are arising; we share them as part of the resonant flow between speaker and listener, while tracking and attending to the speaker's expression.

Dialogues for Healing may take place over several sessions. Even if only one person is the focus of the Dialogue, we may need time to be present with all that is emerging for that one person. It is possible to hold Dialogues for Healing in which more than one person receives support. If this was the agreement entering the Dialogues, it's helpful to plan whether each person will experience empathic support in one session, or to explicitly choose to focus on one person at a time. Sometimes, after a Dialogue for Healing, the speaker emerges with more clarity about what was important for them and may request shifting focus to another type of Dialogue, such as a Dialogue for Shared Understanding to understand the Actor, or a Dialogue for Solution.

Dialogue for Shared Understanding

A Dialogue for Shared Understanding begins by following the steps of our Core Dialogue, the Dialogue to Be Heard. In a Dialogue for Shared Understanding, we have a clear agreement that all those who are impacted by what occurred— whether as the Receiver or Actor—will have an opportunity to speak about their experience and to be received with some understanding of their needs. The goal of the Dialogue for Shared Understanding is to bring into focus the multiple perspectives that might have been present—from different observations to the wide variety of feelings and needs that were stimulated. We try to humanize each person by surfacing what they understood occurred, the needs they were attempting to meet, the systems that may have contributed to their choice, and the needs and values that are currently most present for them.

In doing so, we can mourn together the unmet needs for everyone—we can acknowledge the multitude of costs as impacting not just one person but the whole community. Even if we only do this much, we already have moved away from a dualistic, judgmental framing of what occurred and moved toward compassion for the impact for all. From this place of compassion, we might also wish to move to a Dialogue for Solution to see if we can find strategies that would attend to the original needs without the tragic cost.

Dialogue for Solution

Participants can recognize the need for a Dialogue for Solution after completing any of the other three Dialogues, or they might choose a Dialogue for Solution with clarity that they wish to find new strategies. Regardless, a Dialogue for Solution begins with the Core Dialogue, ensuring that all who would be impacted by a situation or would be affected by any solution have had their needs identified. In this initial Core Dialogue it's important to surface the needs that have been stimulated for each person, as we want to attend, as much as possible, to the full set of needs that are present. We don't necessarily need each person to speak. Having heard others speak, a participant might conclude that their experience has already been represented in what was shared and that the needs they were holding were also named and acknowledged by the group. The goal is inclusion of all the needs, rather than necessarily hearing all voices.

Once we have gathered the needs, we summarize them to be sure we are all on the same page about what the solution we are crafting is trying to address. We then can brainstorm the strategies or actions we can take that would attend to the needs. In this stage we are clear that we are looking for strategies that include all needs. If violence or harm occurs as the result of someone's attempt to meet their needs, leaving their needs out of any solution will only result in them trying even harder to get those needs met, at perhaps greater cost. In our commitment to Beloved Community we want to attend to the needs of all, including those who have received harm and those who have taken actions that resulted in harm.

While our goal is to stretch toward a solution that attends to everyone's needs, sadly it is often outside our capacity to find that solution. Sometimes limited resources prevent us from finding or implementing a truly inclusive solution. Even then, we can strive to collaboratively choose a solution rather than impose it on someone. Sometimes we simply can't conceive of a feasible strategy. In this case we return to the other tenets of the Authentic Dialogues framework. As we acknowledge that white supremacy ideology and other forms of oppression exist, we also place a high value on mitigating their effects through an equitable distribution of resources—giving more where the need is greatest. This can help us navigate how to choose from several imperfect strategies.

After choosing the strategy, we continue to dialogue about possible barriers. What might get in the way of the implementation of this strategy? When and how shall we follow up to assess whether the implementation happened and, if it did, whether it attended to all the needs as intended? What agreements can we make in case someone is unable to follow through with their steps? Given life's unpredictability, planning for failure can interrupt any tendency to assume the failure was from lack of caring for our needs and motivate us to keep looking for new solutions.

In sharing the Authentic Dialogue framework, my hope is that you can see how our commitment to Beloved Community guides the dialogues that can bring people together in the face of conflict and harm. A dear friend and co-mentor, Miki Kashtan, often uses Dawna Markova's phrase to "risk your significance."[3] When we risk our significance, we trust that our experience matters to other people and that our needs are of equal importance in our community. "Risking our significance" means standing up to be seen and heard as we seek to make a difference, individually as well as for the collective community. Change is then possible.

It's not easy. When we participate in Authentic Dialogues, we are resisting generations of programming that dictates who gets to speak, who matters, what's possible. It takes a fierce commitment to the ultimate vision of Beloved Community—a willingness to take responsibility for our biases and programming, to open to new perspectives, to trust in our mattering, and to keep moving with curiosity and vulnerability toward people we may have been told are our enemies. It may not be easy, but we make it more possible with each attempt. In Chapter 8 we'll see how to apply Authentic Dialogues to a common challenge emerging from white supremacy ideology—responding to microaggressions.

NOTES

1. Erica Sherover-Marcuse, "Liberation Theory: A Working Framework," Radical Resilience Institute, p. 1, https://drive.google.com/file/d/1nzMWyo5htEODgHiTy5knF3oiGdKU5xA7/view (accessed September 15, 2022).

2. "The King Philosophy—Nonviolence365®," Martin Luther King Jr. Center for Nonviolent Social Change, February 25, 2022, https://thekingcenter.org/about-tkc/the-king-philosophy/.

3. Aelita Kapitonovna (Dawna) Markova, *I Will Not Die an Unlived Life: Reclaiming Purpose and Passion* (Berkeley, CA: Conari Press, 2000), 2.

8

Microaggressions

This chapter explores how to apply the Authentic Dialogue framework to respond to an all-too-common manifestation of a belief in white supremacy—microaggressions. The word "microaggression" was first coined by Dr. Chester Pierce in the 1970s and brought to mainstream attention through the work of Dr. Derald Wing Sue and his colleagues, who defined them as "brief and commonplace daily verbal, behavioral, or environmental indignities, whether intentional or unintentional, that communicate hostile, derogatory, or negative racial slights and insults toward people of color."[1]

Extensive research has explored the impact of microaggressions on the people who experience them. After reviewing 138 studies published between 2007 and 2020, researchers Lisa B. Spanierman, D. Anthony Clark, and Yeeun Kim concluded that experiencing microaggressions has been associated with adverse psychological effects such as traumatic stress, anxiety, and depression as well as adverse physiological impacts such as hypertension, increased cortisol levels, insomnia, and somatic symptoms such as headaches and stomachaches.[2] They also cite research that demonstrated

that even though microaggressions often present as relational, indirect, social, and even unintentional behaviors,
their adverse impacts are similar to that of physical behaviors
that people readily agree are forms of aggression and thus
warrant being defined as aggressions as well.[3] These findings
are an antidote to a common misperception that only those
who are oversensitive or thin-skinned experience impact
from microaggressions. Given the degree of harm, why are
they called microaggressions? Many researchers point out
that the term is not meant to imply that the impact is small.
Instead, the term "microaggression" is used to describe actions that take place between individuals and are contrasted
with "macroaggressions"—which describe actions that impact groups such as policies and laws.

In *Caste: The Origins of Our Discontents*, Isabel Wilkerson
identifies an essential purpose of microaggressions—they
(un)consciously reinforce the subordinate social position, or
caste, of various groups in society.[4] Wilkerson describes the
caste system upon which US society has operated since before
its founding. Black people were assigned to the lowest caste
and white people to the highest caste. Members of other ethnic groups were assigned to castes in the middle. Laws, social
norms, and expectations were determined at birth, based on
our race and ethnicity, many aspects of our lives—including
where we lived, who we loved, and what labor we performed.
When we encounter someone who defies the (un)conscious
expectations we would have for a person of their caste, microaggressions serve to reinforce caste norms. They remind
the transgressing person that someone from their caste is
not supposed to have an advanced degree, or live in certain
places, or shop in certain stores. Operating via cognitive bias,

caste norms are activated, which stimulate actions that either give voice to surprise that the person is departing from caste norms and marks them as an exception ("You are so articulate!") or attempt to return them to caste-appropriate behavior ("Let me show you where the sale items are").

Dr. Monnica Williams offers a definition of racial microaggressions that is congruent with Wilkerson's framing of microaggressions as a tool that upholds beliefs about white supremacy. Williams describes microaggressions as "deniable acts of racism that reinforce pathological stereotypes and inequitable social norms."[5] Let's unpack this definition. First, Dr. Williams describes microaggressions as deniable acts. When we say "acts," we include both acts of commission (such as explicit name calling or a physician insisting an Indigenous person is lying about not abusing alcohol) and acts of omission (such as a clerk choosing not to serve a Global Majority person while serving white people, or a white person sitting silently next to a Global Majority person rather than introducing themselves). The deniable part speaks to a classic challenge with microaggressions.

Often, people are not even aware that they are engaging in behavior that might be experienced as a microaggression. The person who sits next to someone of the Global Majority at a party but doesn't engage with them, only to get up and introduce themselves animatedly to a white person standing nearby might defend their behavior by saying "I didn't see them" or "I just wanted to get up and move around." As we know, cognitive biases and unconscious stereotypes can shape our perceptions and behavior—they are the driver of microaggressions. They are also the driver of denial. A lack of awareness of our biases combined with societal norms condemning racism means that people often identify plausible, more prosocial explanations for their behavior and deny any possibility that cognitive biases are at play.

Dr. Williams's definition identifies the reinforcement of pathological stereotypes and inequitable social norms as an essential function of microaggressions. Microaggressions inherently arise from the internalization of values promulgated by social structures that marginalize some groups and label their members as "less than." It is thus important to recognize the difference between microaggressions and bias. Because microaggressions are rooted in beliefs that some groups are less than others, a critical understanding of microaggressions includes that they target members of groups that have historically been marginalized and given less structural power in society. In other words, racial microaggressions, for example, are not experienced by white people. Similarly, gender-based microaggressions are not experienced by cisgender men.

Bias underlies acts that target members of a specific group. All microaggressions are examples of bias, but not all acts of bias are microaggressions. A white person at a party ignores the Black person standing near them whom they don't know. Looking around for someone with whom to connect, they walk past the Black person and introduce themselves to the nearest white person, possibly committing a microaggression. The Black person occupies an identity that is marginalized in US society, and the white person's actions may arise out of stereotypes about Black people. A Black person seeing a white person at a party who also takes the same act of avoiding the white person and looking for a Black person to speak to could be committing acts of bias. The Black person may hold prejudice against the white person and white people as a group.

However, since whiteness is not historically marginalized in US society, this act would be an act of bias but not a micro-aggression. Of course, many white people have identities that are historically marginalized, such as being neurodivergent, LGBTQ, or female. White people can thus experience micro-aggressions targeting their historically marginalized iden-tity—for example, acts that are ableist, heteronormative, or sexist. But they cannot experience racial microaggressions. In writing this, I am not condoning acts of bias directed toward members of dominant groups. Neither microaggressions nor acts of bias contribute to the creation of Beloved Community that is my goal. When talking about racial microaggressions, however, it is important to differentiate between individual instances of bias and acts that arise from and, as Dr. Williams notes, continue to reinforce white supremacy beliefs and other systemic inequities.

Let's look at an example of a microaggression a colleague experienced. After more than a decade first as a field opera-tive and then district manager in several countries, Parvathi, a dark-skinned woman of South Asian origin, was recruited to be the director of regional operations for a large multinational organization. After arriving in the region, she traveled from city to city to introduce herself to the staff. At one location the local leaders had arranged a dinner, inviting more than fifty staff from different sites in the area to meet her. As the dinner began, Christopher, a Black man who was the area's finance director, stood up. The room quieted and Christopher said: "Welcome, Parvathi. I want you to tell us your education and list all the jobs you've had before you came here."

Parvathi remembered angrily thinking: "They would not ask me that if I were a tall, white guy. But here I am, a small-framed, South Asian heritage, young-looking woman. I could just tell him off." But instead, Parvathi shared her educational background, then listed the numerous places she had worked. And as the extensive list mounted, the finance director said "Okay" and sat down and the dinner continued. This situation embodies many of the characteristics and challenges of microaggressions. At the time, Parvathi guessed that because she is South Asian and female, both identities that have been historically marginalized, her expertise and experience were being questioned. It's important to note that in this example, Christopher is also a member of a historically marginalized group. The Actor committing a microaggression can be from groups that have been historically dominant or historically marginalized. Sadly anyone, from any background, can internalize the beliefs and stereotypes of white supremacy ideology that underlie microaggressions. Christopher's identity as a Black person does not protect him from exposure to white supremacy beliefs or from acting upon them.

Another challenge those faced with microaggressions encounter is the uncertainty about the motivation for the act. In this case, Parvathi wondered if Christopher's public ask for her credentials stemmed from his belief that women and South Asians would not have the expertise in the field that she did. However, she also entertained other possibilities. She remembered wondering if prior regional directors had not been qualified. Perhaps Christopher was asking this because he wanted reassurance that this time the people chosen to lead them had the necessary experience. The identification of other rationales often proves confusing for those who experience microaggressions. Even as we experience impact, even as we worry if this is yet another time when we are being judged based on our group identity, we may question if our perception is true. Many people report that uncertainty about motivation leads them to believe that they should not address the microaggression or mention the impact they experienced because it would not be fair to the Actor or because they, the Receiver, would be deemed to be the problem. This is one instance where our understanding of the levels of observation can be helpful.

Christopher's actions may or may not have been rooted in white supremacy beliefs or gender bias. Whether or not they were, Parvathi and, as she later learned, other women who were present, were still impacted by what Christopher did. The impact for these women and for Parvathi occurred at the internal and systemic layers of observation. During this interaction Parvathi was reminded of other acts of bias, explicitly because of her ethnicity and gender, that she had experienced at other workplaces. Experiencing actions that could have their origins in the same forms of bias stimulated memories of these past experiences and her awareness of the patterns of bias that exist in society. Christopher's act brought up these memories whether or not he intended Parvathi to experience that impact. The subsequent uncertainty about the degree of welcome and trust Parvathi experienced warrants attention, regardless of Christopher's intention. And Christopher would be served by learning how his request had an impact that was experienced as falling within the field of white supremacy ideology and patriarchy.

Separating an Actor's intention from impact on the Receiver is an essential skill for everyone when microaggressions occur, whether they witness, receive, or commit them. I've seen Actors worry that if a person says their action is a racial microaggression, it also means that the person is saying the Actor intended to do something racist, or is even asserting that the Actor is racist. Actors holding that assumption often respond by collapsing into shame and self-judgment or turning to anger and pushing back against that labeling. In both responses the focus shifts to the Actor's intention—either determining if the Actor was deliberately being racist or acknowledging and mourning the Actor's intentions that did not materialize. This focus on intention takes the place of prioritizing remaining with the impact on the Receiver. I'm inviting us all to consider a third option—prioritizing attending to the Receiver's impact while welcoming the Actor's engagement with self-care or empathy from other sources to support the Actor's capacity to remain present with the Receiver.

We create greater possibilities for healing when both Parvathi, the Receiver, and Christopher, the Actor, acknowledge a microaggression occurred and choose to focus on care for the impact. In doing so, Parvathi can be fully seen for her experience and agreements can be made to address the impact and to prevent recurrences. This does not preclude Christopher, and Parvathi, if she chooses, from also acknowledging his intention. When we separate intention from impact, Christopher can hold himself with self-compassion, recognizing and empathizing with the needs he was attempting to meet instead of taking on the role of the "bad person." Doing so can allow Christopher to take in the full impact on Parvathi. He can remind himself: "Parvathi's pain does not mean I'm a bad person. I don't have to defend myself against it. I can mourn to myself the intention I had in taking the action I did. And while I do so, I can also fully mourn the pain that was stimulated for Parvathi." Christopher's ability to hold both his intention and the impact can make it possible for a double mourning to occur. He can mourn the needs that were unmet related to his original intention and simultaneously mourn the unmet needs Parvathi experienced.

This stance of recognizing the Actor's intention can also be healing for the Receiver. I caution against any demand that the Receiver do so, however. I want this to fully be the Receiver's choice, coming out of awareness of their needs. All too often, there is a demand for the Receiver to recognize the Actor's intention in order for the Actor to experience the relief of being seen, no matter the cost to the Receiver. Instead, I advocate that the Receiver assess their capacity for curiosity about the Actor's intention. In this case, if Parvathi has not yet experienced that impact was addressed, and does not have trust that the impact will be addressed, she may choose to continue to advocate for care for the impact. If she does trust the impact is or will be attended to, understanding Christopher's intention might provide some additional healing or relief for Parvathi.

For many of us, when we experience pain from someone's actions, we fit the actions into preexisting patterns or stories. As we have seen, this can amplify the pain and hopelessness we feel. When we gain information about someone's intentions, we are better able to discern where on the spectrum of intentional racism to unwitting impact their action fits. This information can help Parvathi estimate the degree of risk continuing to engage with Christopher might involve, so she can choose which needs she wishes to attend to. Understanding Christopher's intentions can help Parvathi balance care for needs such as protection, self-care, and effectiveness with other needs such as transformation, hope, and community.

Some folks worry that when we don't insist on an admission of racist intention, we are letting the Actor off the hook. I often hear "They need to admit to what they did" or "Change won't come if they keep saying they didn't mean it." I believe the strategy of getting the Actor to admit that racism was beneath their actions or that they intended the harm that was stimulated is an attempt to ensure impact or harm is acknowledged, and to contribute to trust that there is a commitment to repair present harm and change future behavior. So many times when Receivers try to get support for impact, they are told "They didn't mean it. You should just get over it." Essentially, unless one can prove that intent was there, impact is not acknowledged, much less attended to. When we assert that *the existence of impact is a sufficient reason on its own* to intervene and address acts of microaggression, we move away from the dualistic, right-wrong thinking that contributes to disconnection. Choosing to prioritize attending to impact allows us to stand in a place of nuance and complexity that strengthens our belief in our mattering, centers the experience of the Receiver, and works to mitigate impact in the future.

Although Parvathi was clear that she was impacted by Christopher's request, whether or not it originated from his belief that women of the Global Majority were not qualified, she struggled to navigate another aspect of white supremacy culture. Despite her anger at the request, Parvathi still chose to comply. She struggled with the familiar Catch-22 of responding to microaggressions. If she spoke up and addressed the microaggression itself, she worried that the staff, who did not yet know her, would judge her harshly. Would they think she was overly sensitive, would they be afraid to speak authentically about their worries, would she burn the bridges she had just begun to construct? If Parvathi went along and met Christopher's request, she worried that she was on some level legitimizing the underlying premise of his request—there is a reason to question the credentials of women of color. Torn between wanting to foster goodwill and her longing for dignity and respect, Parvathi chose to publicly share her credentials even as she mourned a sense that she was letting herself down.

Many of us who are Receivers of microaggressions find ourselves in this dilemma where it seems there are just two options, both unbearably costly. We can choose a response that advances negative peace—minimizing or ignoring the impact we experience to avoid conflict or judgment. We purchase that peace with our self-esteem and our sense of mattering, along with other unmet needs. Or we choose to speak up about the microaggression and worry that we are risking our belonging in the group. Some describe wanting to speak up to be known for their experience. However, they worry that the effort it will take to establish shared reality in order to be received with empathy, especially if the Actor's and Bystander's experience is quite different than theirs, will be a costly drain on energy. They choose between accepting the loneliness arising from unmet needs of understanding and care or taking on the exhaustion of persisting to meet needs of shared reality and awareness of impact.

I don't have a one-size-fits-all response. When we are the Receiver, I want us to consider the full array of needs we seek to attend to, both current ones and those related to the creation of Beloved Community, and decide where we have the energy and willingness to proceed. We can accept with compassion and understanding Parvathi's decision to share her credentials in response to Christopher's request as a way to meet her needs for belonging and creation of community. We can have the same compassionate acceptance if she had decided to meet needs for authenticity and respect and challenge the underlying premise of the request rather than address it. Only the Receiver can decide what will serve them most. The rest of us can offer acceptance, support, and any intuitive guidance we are asked for or that comes to us, with great humility—all while staying away from telling anyone what's theirs to do.

When I interviewed Parvathi about her experience for this book, we explored how she might have used the Authentic Dialogue framework to respond. We invited another colleague who had been at that dinner to take the role of Christopher in a dialogue. Parvathi stated that she would still choose to address Christopher's request publicly but would then ask for a private dialogue later the next day. She wanted a Dialogue of Shared Understanding, because although she wanted Christopher to understand the impact she experienced, she was also genuinely curious about both his motivation in making the request and his understanding about dynamics of racism and sexism. Here is that Dialogue.

Authentic Dialogue: Parvathi and Christopher

PARVATHI: I'm wondering if you're open to talking about your question for a minute. I'd like to share what came up for me hearing your request, and I'm also curious where your request is coming from. I would like us to have mutual understanding since we're going to be working together.

CHRISTOPHER: Sure.

PARVATHI: I would like you to know that in my career, in my professional life, I've had what seems like a similar experience repeated many times where I come in to do a job and people question my experience. They don't seem to believe that I have the qualifications needed. I guess a couple of things that come up for me are, well, how would I be here otherwise? Why would you doubt it? It seems like it's related to the color of my skin, and my gender, and often my age, that people can't believe that somebody with that combination could have the amount of experience it would take to do this job. So, hearing all of that, I'm wondering if you could tell me what you're getting from what I said.

CHRISTOPHER: Well, you were saying that this has happened to you a lot. This isn't the first time you've had someone question your qualifications. And you're thinking that it has to do with who you are, like your age and your gender and the color of your skin. That this is where this is coming from.

PARVATHI: Thanks for reflecting that back. And I guess, hearing that you got the gist of what I said, I'm curious what comes up in you hearing me share?

CHRISTOPHER: Yeah, I mean, I didn't want to hurt your feelings or anything. I just wanted to make sure that headquarters was sending us someone who could do the job because in the past they haven't. People come that aren't qualified, that don't know what they're doing.

PARVATHI: Well, I want to ask you, did you ask that question of the last people who came? I know the directors before me were white men, so did you ask them that question?

CHRISTOPHER: Yeah, honestly, no. I didn't ask the other directors the same question. I mean, I don't know why I didn't, but I just wanted to get to know you and feel comfortable working together. And I just thought asking straight out might be a way.

PARVATHI: Well, I can see this piece you're bringing, Christopher, about wanting to make sure we're not being screwed by headquarters, essentially. That you're trying to support the team by making sure the team is in good hands?

CHRISTOPHER: Yeah.

PARVATHI: But you're asking me this publicly when you haven't asked anyone else who came before me. So for me, I worry that you're also undermining trust in the group for me, the person who's going to be leading them. It would have been possible for you to ask me the same question one on one.

CHRISTOPHER: Well. Hmm, I'm just trying to think of why I was asking it publicly. I mean, I wanted to stand up for the group. I want everyone to know that it matters to me who comes here to talk to us and give us advice and help us. It matters that someone's going to stand up and say, hey, we want them to think about what we need rather than just sending us whoever.

PARVATHI: So I get that you're wanting a sense of trust in who's coming to do the job and for your colleagues to understand that you've got their back. And asking me what you did in front of everybody, the cost of that was at my expense. I worry that you raising questions about my qualifications might lead people to think the regional leadership doesn't trust me.

CHRISTOPHER: Yeah, are you worried it might make it harder to build relationships and get people to trust your leadership if they think we don't?

PARVATHI: Yeah. I think it does make my job harder, especially coming in as the first woman you all have had as a leader. And, in addition to that, I wonder if the other women, especially the women of color on your team, may have seen it as you acting at my expense. That you were putting down another woman of color rather than celebrating a woman of color coming in, in a position of leadership.

CHRISTOPHER: Hmm. I know there was some surprise about having a regional director who was a woman of color. Some of the women were excited about meeting you.

PARVATHI: Yeah. It's part of why I wanted to speak up, for all of us. It's part of this system that we're in, that women and women of color like me get this message over and over again that we're not good enough. And I would love in our workplace if we can start transforming that assumption to show that it's not the case—so everyone knows their value is seen and appreciated.

CHRISTOPHER: I don't want to give anyone the message that I don't trust their skills, especially because they are women. I know how hard all our staff work, even without enough resources. And I know what it's like to have people assume I'm not good enough because I'm Black.

PARVATHI: Yeah. I was honestly more shocked hearing that request coming from you because I thought you would have the same understanding of how hard it is to repeatedly have to prove yourself in spaces where you're the only person of color in a leadership role.

CHRISTOPHER: Hmm. I'm seeing it wasn't just me asking you to list out your credentials, but how much you're tired of doing this when you go to new sites, and the added layer of hopelessness or frustration you felt when the person asking you was someone you were hoping would have some shared understanding and be supportive?

PARVATHI: Yeah. I was really hoping things would be different since so many people on the team are Black and Brown.

CHRISTOPHER: And I'm also getting how much you're wanting to model something different for the women of color here, to have this office be part of the transformation that we're working toward?

PARVATHI: Yes. It's not just about me, but what it means for the work we're doing. I feel a little more relief. I'm really appreciating that we've had the chance to talk about it and come to some shared understanding both in terms of where we're coming from and in terms of the impact on the larger group and the environment we're trying to create in our workplace. My read is that you've been kind of impacted by our conversation. And because it was something you asked me in front of everyone, would you be willing to share with the group that impact or what you're taking away from this conversation at our next meeting?

CHRISTOPHER: Yeah. I can.

PARVATHI: Okay, thanks. It's really important to me that we're clear on what the big takeaways are and that we're aligned. Can we meet for lunch next week before the meeting, perhaps for thirty minutes or so?

CHRISTOPHER: Yeah. I'd be happy to.

There are several elements to highlight in this Dialogue. First, I appreciated the numerous connection requests that Parvathi made: briefly checking on Christopher's willingness for dialogue, checking his understanding of what was important to her when she first expressed herself and how he was impacted by what she shared. There were also several empathic exchanges where either Christopher or Parvathi tried to reflect their understanding of what was important to the other person. There is a formal way to do this when following a classical Nonviolent Communication style—one asks "Are you feeling . . . because you are needing. . . ?" In the Dialogue both people modeled how it is possible to have empathic connection flow in a conversational style that might be received as more natural.

For instance, Parvathi said to Christopher: "I can see this piece you're bringing, Christopher, about wanting to make sure we're not being screwed by headquarters, essentially. That you're trying to support the team by making sure the team is in good hands?" She could have easily said more formally: "Were you feeling desperate because you really need support and trust in leadership?" This would likely not be as connecting for Christopher since some people might lose trust that they were fully heard when their specific words and context are stripped from the reflection. Mirroring or closely paraphrasing someone's words is sometimes necessary for them to get that you truly understand the nuances of their specific experience. Parvathi added in enough context and used language that fit the setting since the goal of the Dialogue was to connect and to foster a sense of deep understanding.

One of the functions of the more classical phrasing of Nonviolent Communication is to move us away from the stories and strategies that obscure the needs that unite us. When there is agreement about the relationship between the strategy and the need—for example, "to support the team by making sure the team is in good hands"—we can speak about both since it often helps to facilitate the connection. When agreement is not there, you might choose to move closer to clear needs as shown on the list (see Figure 7 in the Appendix) and classical Nonviolent Communication language to make it more likely that each person can be fully understood.

Parvathi made another choice in the Dialogue that I want to highlight. When she initially brought up her observations to Christopher, he reflected back what he heard and then offered his intention—"I just wanted to make sure that headquarters was sending us someone who could do the job because in the past they haven't." It's really easy to let the introduction of the intention change the direction of the

Dialogue away from the impact Parvathi experienced, and indeed, to have the intention negate Parvathi's experience. Instead of being distracted, Parvathi continued to advocate for the entire picture to be seen, not just the intention, when she asked: "Did you ask that question of the last people who came? I know the directors before me were white men, so did you ask them that question?"

In doing so, Parvathi did not negate Christopher's words or question his intention. She simply returned to naming the external observation that regardless of his intention, he had acted toward her in a way that he had not done to white men. As the conversation proceeded, Parvathi acknowledged Christopher's genuine concern for the integrity of the team and still highlighted the external observations ("You asked me something you did not ask white men before me"), the internal observation ("This is a pattern that I've experienced over and over again"), and the systemic observation ("Women and women of color like me get this message over and over again that we're not good enough"). In doing so, Parvathi was able to walk that nuanced line of naming the observations and connecting them to the impact she received while still occupying a stance that she does not have to know Christopher's intention to do that and that learning his intentions did not negate the impact she experienced.

As you can imagine, this Dialogue asks of the participants a lot of skill and vulnerability. With her only knowledge of Christopher being that he said this thing that fit patterns of racism she had experienced before, Parvathi can still choose to walk toward connection and the possibility of Beloved Community. She also modeled how to avoid some of the challenges of these dialogues, such as shifting the conversation to his intention or even empathizing with the past struggles he had with headquarters. I imagine in an actual dialogue, Christopher would have to persevere through any shame that might come up as he hears Parvathi's experience in order to acknowledge when his behavior was inconsistent with his values. These are some of the challenges we navigate as we use Authentic Dialogues, challenges we'll explore in Chapter 9.

NOTES

1. Monnica T. Williams, "Microaggressions: Clarification, Evidence, and Impact," *Perspectives on Psychological Science* 15, no. 1 (2019): 3–26, https://doi.org/10.1177/1745691619827499. Derald Wing Sue et al., "Racial Microaggressions in Everyday Life: Implications for Clinical Practice," *American Psychologist* 62, no. 4 (2007): 271–286.

2. Lisa B. Spanierman, D. Anthony Clark, and Yeeun Kim, "Reviewing Racial Microaggressions Research: Documenting Targets' Experiences, Harmful Sequelae, and Resistance Strategies," *Perspectives on Psychological Science* 16, no. 5 (2021): 1037–1059.

3. Spanierman, Clark, and Kim, "Reviewing Racial Microaggressions Research."

4. Isabel Wilkerson, *Caste: The Origins of Our Discontents* (New York: Random House, 2020).

5. Williams, "Microaggressions," 4.

9

Rising to the Challenge

Even when we are committed to showing up and participating in antiracist conversations, it can be difficult to navigate some of the challenges that we encounter. We can experience challenges in setting the conditions for the conversation, navigating our internal landscape, and managing the interpersonal connections between ourselves and one or more people. Thinking through and preparing for some of these challenges can help us handle them more effectively when we do face them. Let's use responding to microaggressions as our focus in this chapter since they are so ubiquitous and can illustrate how both Bystanders and Receivers can interrupt harmful behaviors and initiate antiracist conversations.

Before the Conversation

Environment

One challenge to address before beginning a Dialogue relates to our internal and external environment. As much as possible, we aim to create conditions in which authentic conversations can happen. This is much easier to do when we are able to converse outside of a sense of urgency, but sometimes a time-sensitive Dialogue needs to happen. There are a few ways we can support those in-the-moment conversations, so that maximum vulnerability and presence can be achieved. Externally, we must consider time, place, and who is present. It is generally supportive to move the Dialogue away from an audience. The presence of an audience may make it more difficult for both the Receiver and the Actor to be authentic and open to each other.

This is especially true when the audience might be taking sides, which causes both people in the Dialogue to grasp more firmly their ideas of rightness and wrongness as a way of demonstrating allegiance to their group. When away from the group, it may be easier for both people to see each other, to take in the other's needs and to allow themselves to be moved. Sometimes, when harm has happened in a group setting, healing can also happen within the group setting. Yet even then, it can be incredibly helpful for people to first meet in smaller configurations to establish connection and build trust, and then reconvene as a group when there is more openness.

We also want to find a location that is sufficiently neutral. Being mindful about our environments can help us minimize the signs of power that are held by one side or another. For example, it is likely that it will be more difficult for a Receiver to challenge the behavior of an Actor who is their supervisor if the meeting takes place in the supervisor's office, where people are hired or fired (even if it is a facilitated meeting). We want to remove as many barriers as possible for people to be able to speak their truth, even small ones.

We can also attend to our internal environment. While it may seem obvious, it is crucial to pay attention to your physical state before you begin a conversation. Are you trying to have a Dialogue when you have not eaten and your blood sugar is low? Have you been working long hours and are physically exhausted? As much as possible, attempt to provide your body with the care it needs to be in its best operating state. Even if circumstances don't permit—for example, you don't have the resources to meet your basic needs, or there is a crisis occurring that limits access to shelter or rest—small things can make a difference. Two minutes of meditation, stepping outside to breathe in fresh air, drinking a glass of water, using the bathroom—these are small but mighty actions that can bring your body closer to its baseline and help you be more present in your Dialogue. Taking the time to do these things is a gift we can offer ourselves and others, as it also supports us in decreasing our sense of urgency and feeling called into the expansive present.

Urgency

When a microaggression occurs, Bystanders and Receivers often feel some urgency about responding. Both Bystanders and Receivers may worry that if they don't say something right away, the Actor or others may perceive them as accepting or approving of the microaggression. In addition, Receivers may worry that if they choose to raise the issue later, after some time has elapsed, this might make it seem like a bigger deal or suggest they had been stewing about it. Bystanders can be worried about how they are perceived, as either colluding or clueless, if they don't speak up in the moment.

Speaking out of urgency often causes us to speak without clarity about why we are speaking. When we do so, we are more likely to respond from habitual patterns of thinking and conditioning. As the Receiver, urgency to speak may lead us to respond from moralistic judgments—using external dualistic definitions of good and bad to declare the act is wrong, the Actor is therefore bad and deserves to be punished. With time to reflect, however, we might instead choose to respond from an awareness of needs: "This action does not meet needs for me nor others. I want to prioritize stopping the harm and invite the Actor to attend to the harm that was stimulated and to find other strategies for us to both have our needs met in the future."

As the Bystander, responding with urgency may lead us to respond without awareness of the Receiver's needs. Doing so essentially centers, or puts the focus on, what the Bystander needs. When we slow down, we are more likely to notice whether or not the Receiver desires our help, and if so, what form of support would best serve them.

Release the sense of urgency. Many conversations benefit from slowing down rather than rushing in. If, as the Receiver, we want to bring back a topic from even ten years ago, we can. It impacted you, and your wish to revisit it suggests you are still being impacted by it. You can simply say: "I wasn't sure about bringing this up when it first happened. As time passed, I noticed I was still unsettled." Then share the needs you're hoping to meet by bringing it up now. There can be a wide variety of needs. For instance: "I'd like to talk with you about a remark you made at the conference last year. I'm bringing this conversation to you because I think that seeing that you truly understand the different kinds of impact that happened may help me have more trust that we're both committed to learning whatever we need to learn or do to make such events less likely to happen in the future."

Caretaking

Often emerging from a sense of urgency when witnessing a microaggression, a Bystander may feel an urge to protect or take care of the Receiver. I recall as a teen, taking a class with a teacher who repeatedly joked about female students and their bodies and propositioned several students. In a small group meeting one day, the teacher began making his sexist comments. When a young man in the group protested, stating, "You're making her uncomfortable," the teacher turned to me and said, "You know I'm just joking, right, honey. I don't mean anything. Tell him." I quietly said, "It's fine," even though I hated everything that was happening.

The young man's choice to speak up, explicitly naming that he thought I was uncomfortable, was caretaking. I knew how to speak up, had I wanted to do so. I was aware that other attempts to intervene in the moment had not been successful and that other efforts were under way to address the teacher's behavior. In the moment, declaring I was not okay with it would have ended with me becoming a target of this teacher. By speaking up, I could no longer ignore the behavior as I had been doing and continue with the classwork since I needed to graduate. I was instead forced to choose between risking the teacher's enmity or explicitly stating something that was not true that gave permission to the teacher's behavior.

I'm not saying a Bystander should never speak up when they witness harm. I admire the awareness of the young man who spoke up and his willingness to intervene. However, what I would have preferred in that moment is that he checked with me after the group. Checking in with me, letting me know he was prepared to speak up, and giving me the choice of whether I wanted his intervention would have felt supportive. He could also have chosen to interrupt what was happening. Distracting the Actor from the Receiver (e.g., engaging the teacher in a conversation on a different topic) or otherwise drawing the Actor's attention (e.g., dropping a book or spilling a drink) is an intervention Bystanders can use that does not increase the risk for the Receiver and indeed could give the Receiver an opportunity to leave.

When we feel compelled to speak up as a Bystander, naming our own impact, not the Receiver's, is incredibly supportive. I can imagine many needs were not met for the young man—respect, dignity, fairness, learning. He could say to the teacher: "I'd like you to stop. I'm uncomfortable with what you're doing. You have a lot of power as a teacher, and I don't think most of us feel safe telling you we don't like it. I know I feel scared right now. I really just want to learn this stuff I was excited about." The conversation would then be between him and the teacher. I would not have to participate if I did not wish to do so and would not be put on the spot as I was. When we speak up as a Bystander, we must aim to do so from an understanding of our needs, not our assumption, especially without checking, of the Receiver's needs. Knowing our needs before we speak is essential.

Bystanders sometimes worry that any form of speaking could make things worse. They worry how to navigate the complexities of each response. If they respond and clearly name their needs as the motivation for their response, a concern is that it will be received as centering their experience and drawing attention away from the Receiver. If they wait until they can better assess the Receiver's needs, they worry it will be experienced as not caring. This uncertainty of how our actions may be received can lead us to freeze. The Bystander can instead choose to accept this uncertainty and still act. If we understand that there is no single response that works in every situation, the Bystander can slow down, become clear on the needs they are hoping to meet, including those of support and choice for the Receiver, and take action. If the Bystander maintains a stance of curiosity and humility, even as they act, they can assess the impact they are having and shift to be responsive to needs that are emerging.

Global Majority people often navigate the complex uncertainty of these interactions: "How will I be received? Will I be understood? Will I have the impact I'm hoping for?" White supremacy culture can serve to protect white folks from that uncertainty since it shields them from awareness of the impact of their actions or how they are received. Stepping into that uncertainty and managing the ensuing discomfort are ways white Bystanders can work to dismantle white supremacy culture.

During the Conversation

Once we begin the conversation, new challenges emerge.

Misaligned Purpose

A common challenge is the lack of agreement about the purpose of the conversation. This can happen when the purpose was not clarified and agreed upon before the conversation began. It can also happen over the course of the conversation as people's willingness and capacity might shift. For instance, two people might have agreed on a dialogue in which the Receiver, not the Actor, would be heard. As the conversation proceeds, the Actor may be so deeply touched by the Receiver's expression of impact that the Actor energetically moves ahead into a conversation about finding a solution. The Receiver, who still is working on regaining trust with the Actor, might not yet be willing to jump into problem-solving mode.

When purpose becomes misaligned in this way, an explicit check-in of what each person is needing can be extremely helpful. New agreements around a conversation's purpose can be crafted together throughout the course of a conversation. It is important to remember that these encounters are not static, and neither are we. The best way to make sure that both people are continuing to feel agency in the multidirectional flow of a conversation is to stay grounded in what's happening in our own bodies and to check in to see what's happening for the other person. Sometimes this may involve taking a pause, doing a body scan, closing one's eyes, or standing up and then sitting back down. Whenever we re-engage with our body during conversation, it is much more likely that we will be able to stay grounded in what is most true for us and therefore show up in ways that we do not later regret. When we remove our sense of urgency, we allow conversations to take longer and occur over multiple encounters. If new purposes are identified, folks can agree to address them later.

Reactivity and Restimulation

It certainly happens, despite the best of intentions, that a participant in an Authentic Dialogue experiences a restimulation of emotions they experienced when the stimulus first occurred. Defensiveness, or the Listener's inability to reflect the Speaker's experiences, may be interpreted as painful repetitions of exclusion. Alternatively, a person may agree to participate in a conversation despite not being aligned with its purpose. For example, many Receivers of microaggressions are told that as part of creating repair, they must sit down and share their experience, then listen to the other person's experience. Some Receivers agree to this, despite knowing that they do not have a sense of sufficient trust and safety in the setting to be as vulnerable or as open to the other person's experience as the Dialogue needs without there being a cost to themselves. As the conversation proceeds, this lack of trust can cause the Receiver to either freeze or return to prior defensive patterns of attack or submission.

It is crucial to pay attention to your limits as you begin these conversations. Tracking yourself is an important part of Authentic Dialogue. You can do this by trying to notice, as you engage with someone, when you are no longer attuned to what the other person is sharing. Notice when you are mentally (and sometimes verbally) defensively picking apart everything you hear rather than staying in the stance of curiosity. As soon as you notice signs of disconnection or restimulation, take a pause. It can be a short pause—a moment of silence—while you check in with what you're feeling or needing in that moment. This may lead to a longer break, if you realize you need empathic support from other people to reground and reconnect to your intention for being in dialogue.

Demand for Completion

It may be that you realize that an essential limit of yours has been reached and you can no longer engage in any kind of dialogue without new forms of support or some shift in how the other person is showing up. There is no demand that because a Dialogue has begun, it must be finished. Instead, stop and take stock when necessary, then make a decision to continue or not based on the awareness of the needs of all involved.

I had this experience when I agreed to a Dialogue of Shared Understanding with someone who had been repeatedly attempting to bring me into a closer degree of involvement in their personal life than I wanted. Despite my requests for limited forms of contact, they continued to send me long emails and leave me lengthy text and voice messages. As the Dialogue proceeded, I realized that the person did not have the ability to hear what was important to me. I realized this because every time I spoke, they responded with shame and continued to frame my attempt to set agreements as a form of oppression. This person needed a significant amount of empathy for challenges they had experienced in their life before they would have the capacity to hear me or anyone else. Since I was not willing to support them in that type of healing conversation, or to enter a unilateral Dialogue to Be Heard focused on their experience, I shared with them that the limits of my capacity and willingness had been reached. We agreed to end the conversation.

Shame

Shame is another form of reactivity that is commonly experienced in antiracist dialogue. As Receivers, we may feel shame that we "allowed" ourselves to be impacted by someone else's actions, that we did not stand up for ourselves as we wished, or that we responded the way that we did. If feelings of shame come up for you as a Receiver, you can pause. It is hard to express yourself or to hold onto your own experience when shame is high. If you pause for a moment, you may discover that the shame is coming from old patterns and messages left over from receiving the impacts of white supremacy ideology, rather than from anything that you are doing "wrong." You may have a contract (those unconscious internal rules we set for ourselves) to be compliant or not to express your truths. Sometimes it is enough to just acknowledge that an unconscious contract might be there to alleviate its pressure and shame.

As Actors, we may feel shame as we recognize the extent of the impact we had, as we acknowledge how unconscious white supremacy ideas influenced our behavior, or as we fear judgment by others. Shame is often paralyzing, as it forces us inward into a spiral of abusive self-judgment. When shame takes hold like this, we lose our capacity to empathize with ourselves or with others and effective dialogue becomes impossible. As the Actor, we might try to avoid feelings of shame by blaming the other person for our discomfort. We might blame them for our present-moment feelings of shame, or we may even seek to relieve ourselves of any responsibility for the impact they experienced by blaming them for their experience of impact ("You're too sensitive, I was just making a dumb joke, I can't believe you would think that"). All these reactions impede the Authentic Dialogue process.

If feelings of shame come up for you as the Actor, you can also pause. It is okay to let the other person in the conversation know that you need a moment to self-connect to be able to continue with full presence. Turning to self-empathy, you can notice the shame. You can tell yourself: "Ahh, I am feeling shame in this moment." Shame is actually a judgment overlaid onto a feeling of intense regret. You may choose to allow yourself to feel and mourn the action or inaction you regret, and in so doing, connect to the underlying need you did not meet, the value that you so much want to live by. Take a moment to ground in the present. Notice your feet and the surface they are upon. Rub your index and thumb together and notice the sensation this creates. Glance around the room, and let your eyes rest on something that catches your attention. Take a moment to breathe. Then ask yourself what need the shame is trying to meet.

Is shame the strategy you learned that tries to make sure you are paying attention when your actions impact someone, so that you will be motivated to choose a different action? Is shame how you've learned to show someone that you feel sorrow as you see their pain? Is shame the way you can reassure yourself that you truly don't align with racist values and ideas? As you connect to the need, take a moment to sit with it. You can repeat to yourself something like this: "Shame is my body's sign of how much I value learning to reduce harmful impact. When I feel this way, it's because of how deeply I long to move through the world from an antiracist stance. It's okay to make mistakes and impact other people negatively; I am a creature who is worthy of love and always growing."

Remind yourself that in returning to the dialogue, you are taking new actions to create repair and better align with your values. Check in after this moment of self-empathy. Are you able to return to the Dialogue and offer your attention and presence to the other person? If you are still unable to do so, consider taking a longer break. Check in with the other person to see if they can agree to a longer pause, and make an agreement on when to reconvene. Make sure to take care of yourself during the longer pause, so that you show up fully for the reconvening.

Demanding Care from the Receiver

In addition, when racialized harm has occurred, an Actor who turns to the Receiver for emotional support with their shame may be putting the Receiver in an incredibly challenging position. One postulate of white supremacy culture is that Global Majority people must ignore any impact they receive from a white person and instead prioritize the well-being of the white person. This isn't ever said explicitly, and yet it's ever present. If a Receiver experienced an impact from a white person, asking them to put aside that impact to tend to the white person's shame is tragically reminiscent of white supremacy culture's deep devaluation of the feelings and needs of Global Majority people.

This is the one reason why, unsurprisingly, when white people present with tears of guilt and shame as they recognize the impact of their behavior, especially if they are then unable to maintain focus on the experiences of the person they impacted, many Global Majority people fiercely resist the implicit demand to offer care. If you are the Actor, take a break for self-empathy, or turn to your community for empathy, instead of asking the Receiver to empathize with your shame.

Empathy Blocks

I define "empathy" as the act of reflecting back the feelings and needs of another person in an attuned way. This can occur in two different forms throughout an Authentic Dialogue: through healing empathy and functional empathy. Healing empathy is a mode of empathy whose goal is to support our depth of connection to what we value. This kind of empathy can lead to profound shifts in our understanding of ourselves or others. As we practice healing empathy, we continue to reflect back what we hear, unpeeling layer after layer of needs as we do so. With this purpose, healing empathy may take place over a lengthy period of time—occurring over the course of multiple sessions and many months, for instance. Our focus here is on the depth of connection.

Alternatively, there is functional empathy. The goal of functional empathy is to support the ability to reengage with one's purpose in the moment. In an Authentic Dialogue we might say: "I am agreeing to be in dialogue so that this person can be heard." As we listen, we may hear something that is challenging to us. For example, perhaps hearing another person's experience, we feel so flooded by anger that we are no longer able to be present to the speaker. Or we may experience such dismay at the gap in perspective between us and the speaker that we get lost in despair and lose connection with them. A brief pause for functional empathy or self-empathy can support us in connecting with the needs our anger or despair may be pointing to. Perhaps the anger points to the fierceness of our longing for protection for all bodies. Maybe our despair is the urgency we feel to experience shared reality and the understanding it engenders.

With this newly rediscovered awareness, we can choose to hold that fierceness or urgency in our consciousness and return to hearing the other person's experience. We don't, in that moment, need to unpeel the layers of our longing for protection for all bodies, or to express our deep mourning that this need is so far from being met for so many humans. This is not because these longings are not important: it is because voicing them, in this moment, will shift the focus of the Dialogue and not allow the speaker to receive the attention and focus that they had asked for. Becoming aware of our needs for mourning and justice, we can make an agreement with ourselves to tend to these needs at another time and continue to meet our needs for contribution and connection by resuming the present Dialogue. The key element of functional empathy is that it is as brief as possible. As we gain skills in empathy and self-empathy, we will find even one minute of self-connection can be enough to return us to presence. It can be helpful to track the content that stimulates you when you are in Dialogue, then set aside time for empathy and self-empathy when you are not actually in the Dialogue. This could help you more quickly understand your needs if the topic itself is one that typically is hard for you to hear.

Empathic connection is a fundamental part of Authentic Dialogue, and it can also be quite a challenge. Both too much and too little empathy can take place. Sometimes during the Dialogue someone becomes stimulated. They may have an intense reaction to something they heard—despair, anger, grief, shame. When we talk about racism, we can quickly tap into the absolute horrors that humankind is capable of. Experiencing strong emotions during conversations about the impact of racism makes sense and indeed is somewhat predictable. One response to these emotions is empathy. If the person sharing their impact is the one who is expressing the emotion, staying in empathic connection with them can help to deepen their sense that the fullness of their experience was understood. Yet if I am in dialogue with you and I don't agree with the facts of what you are saying, I may not be able to respond with empathy when you break down in tears. I may respond with too little empathy to support a sense of connection. On some level, this may be because I am worried that by empathizing with you, you will take this as a sign that I not only understand your perspective, but I also agree that your perspective is the true one. Authentic Dialogue is predicated on the exact opposite understanding—it assumes people have divergent viewpoints.

The purpose of Authentic Dialogue is to facilitate the mutual exchange and understanding of these perspectives, not to get everyone to adopt the perspective of one person. Even with this understanding, it can still be challenging to get our brains to relax and trust that we are not being asked to deny our own truth when we empathize with another person's truth. One small strategy that can be helpful when we notice our resistance arise is to say something like this: "I notice that we have a very different understanding about this piece. I can share my perspective later, but right now, I'm really curious and want to understand more about your experience." Doing so, especially if we make and keep a commitment to ourselves that we will have a turn to share our own experience, can make it possible for us to choose empathy again.

Too Much Empathy

We can also respond with too much empathy! I acknowledge that it seems there is no such thing as too much empathy—we need a lot more empathy in our world. But sometimes, in a specific encounter, we can respond with too much empathy for our purpose. If we are in a Dialogue for Shared Understanding, where both people are planning to share their experience, we have to be careful not to use all of our meeting's allotted time for empathizing with just one person. Sometimes this can occur because the person who is receiving empathy is operating from a large empathy deficit. They may have never spoken about their experience or may have never been met with empathy.

When they receive empathy and respond with emotional intensity (e.g., bursting into loud tears, experiencing bodily tremors, etc.), those offering empathy are uncertain how to respond. They worry that the depth of emotion being expressed means the speaker's need is huge and thus should be prioritized over their own need. The person offering empathy may be afraid that interrupting this part of the empathic exchange might be perceived as them not properly caring for the other person's pain. Yet if we don't make sure to make space for both people's experience, then the person who does not get to share their experience may walk away from the conversation feeling depleted, resentful, and unheard. It is crucial, for the success of this type of Authentic Dialogue, for both people to be allowed to share and receive empathy.

If you are finding it difficult to shift focus to yourself, in the face of so much emotion from the other person, it can be helpful to preface the shift by naming why it is of value to you. You might say something like: "I am so moved by what you've shared of how overwhelming this conflict was for you. I now have a strong sense of how many things have contributed to the deep pain about exclusion you have. As I notice the time, I'm tracking that we had agreed to allot time so that we both can share our experience to build understanding. I really want to keep that agreement. If we paused here and took a moment of silence to sit with all that's come up for you, would you be able to switch focus and hear more of my experience when we resume?"

Insistence on Equality

The belief that we can productively undo racism by treating everyone equally from this point forward can undermine attempts to truly attend to needs via Authentic Dialogue. It is important to understand that "equality" is not a human need; rather, it is a strategy for attempting to meet human needs. This might show up in dialogue when someone insists that both Actor and Receiver get equal time to be heard by the other. A white Actor might resist agreeing to be in a Dialogue to Be Heard when the Receiver says: "I don't have the capacity to hear you right now. Are you willing to hear what came up for me in response to your action and reflect back what you are getting so I can trust I was understood? I ask this with the understanding that if you need support or to be heard yourself after we talk, I don't anticipate being the one to offer it, so I hope that you can turn to your community for that kind of support."

In these cases, people sometimes state: "If we only listen to Global Majority people, that's another form of racism!" Asking for equality, no matter the context, without consideration of any other needs can end up being another way of centering whiteness. When we do this, we are prioritizing the white person's needs for understanding and to be seen at a cost to the Global Majority person's need for trust and safety. Instead of this race-blind equality, we must take into consideration all the various ways that harm has happened and continues to happen in our world. One form of harm that I've seen happen many times is the repeated experience of being in interracial interactions where the needs of white people are attended to first, and the needs of Global Majority folks, even if acknowledged, are dropped because there were not sufficient resources to attend to both.

Another form of harm that I've seen occur happens due to constrained choice. Many Global Majority folks report the experience of agreeing to enter a dialogue or to empathize with their white peers, even when they are exhausted and have little hope of mutuality. This is often because Global Majority folks are afraid of the judgment and social and professional consequences that they may experience if they are not immediately available for dialogue. Both instances occur as manifestations of a white supremacy culture that unconsciously prioritizes the needs of white people over those of Global Majority people. In such cases, we want to do our best to be aware of this pattern and to minimize its occurrence. We can do this by helping the white person access the support they want to have (they might have needs for empathy, to be heard, or to be seen) with the understanding that those needs can be met by many people, not only by the Global Majority person who was harmed. These are a few of the strategies, besides equality, that we can explore to meet our different needs. In this way we include needs around choice and transformation of patterns of oppression while still attending to needs for care for all.

Overwhelm

As I write about these challenges, I recognize that this is not an exhaustive list. I acknowledge that they may seem overwhelming! We might feel hopeless about ever achieving a degree of ease in entering these dialogues, ever gaining a sense of fluidity. This sense of overwhelm is indeed the last challenge I'll address in this chapter. We did not have to consciously learn how to relate to each other, how to talk, how to judge each other or whose needs to prioritize (our own, if we are white; or white people's needs, if we are of the Global Majority). The pervasiveness of white supremacy culture showing us how to do this has meant that we have been absorbing those lessons, in almost every interaction or through global media, throughout our entire lives. It makes white supremacy culture seem as natural as all the things most of us learn without conscious effort—how to eat, how to breathe, how to move around, how to communicate using the language of our community.

And yet, I promise: there are a lot of things we can learn to such a degree of mastery that it can feel as effortless as breathing. When my children were younger, they enjoyed skateboarding. I watched their attempts to use their skateboards in the beginning—wobbly efforts to consciously balance, which led to many overcorrections and falls. I watched every small bump in the road or unexpected hazard that led to a tumble. But they were determined to master skateboarding. Over and over again, they tried. And tried. Balancing became as natural as walking, their bodies shifting without thought as they flew with such grace down all the roads of our city. Falls became fewer as they subconsciously noticed potholes and bumps in the road and effortlessly navigated around them. What was once a scary goal for them became as natural as walking.

Using this consciousness and choosing this form of dialogue is the same. It will seem so much harder, just like skateboarding was infinitely harder than walking. But with perseverance and commitment to the larger goal, Authentic Dialogues and an antiracist lens can become your new natural. In our last chapter we explore the essential role awareness and vision play in helping us overcome the constraints of human biology, white supremacy beliefs, and anti-Blackness in order to work toward Beloved Community.

10

Paving the Path

During most of my life as an activist, I felt that if
oppressed people could just get the power, things
would get better. Shifting the power, flipping the
power, is not really changing things systemically.
What it does is reenact dehumanization. One of the
most powerful things we can do to heal from racism
is to let go of the rage and reach for the intimacy.

—LILLIAN ROYBAL ROSE

Lillian Roybal Rose's words succinctly point to the vision of
this book.[1] With this work we seek to find a way to dismantle white supremacy culture. By "dismantling," I mean being
able to reject all of the beliefs and ideas and practices that
have dehumanized all people: both those of the Global Majority and those who are white. A system that turns human
beings into chattel is not a system that serves life. A system
that enslaves and murders human beings without thought
is not a system that serves life. A system that desensitizes
human beings, methodically takes human babies and strips
them of their hard-wired drives for compassion and empathy
in order to preserve the status quo that upholds white supremacy beliefs, is not a system that serves life. A system that

makes it possible for people to see other humans suffer and not act is not a system that serves life. I don't want to change *who* the system is serving, I want to dismantle it entirely. In such a system, no one is truly served, whether they are in the putative power-up or power-down position.

This vision—of a society that is rooted in connection and a deep value for all life—has been seen in communities from generations past to today, in all corners of the Earth. I believe it is a vision that resonates with our true essence as human beings. This essence leads babies to offer everyone around them some of their fruit that they find delicious. This essence led people living in the early years of the United States to resist the false narratives about Black people being cursed or seen as animals, and try to help them escape from enslavement, despite huge risk to themselves. This essence leads people today to come together and stand, arms linked, in protest against the continued murders of Global Majority people in cities worldwide.

The insidious reach of white supremacy culture into every system of modern life is an attempt to extract this essence out of us, and replace it with one of separation, scarcity, and judgment. To reconnect to that essence, we need to do more than just change our behavior: we need to change our understanding of everyone's behavior and find new models for action. In my own life I have found nonviolence and Nonviolent Communication to be powerful tools that have made it possible to resist white supremacy culture. The commitment to nonviolence stands in direct opposition to white supremacy culture's beliefs. It is a fierce commitment to be unrelenting in our resistance to oppressive systems (both internal and external), without enacting harm ourselves. It is a commitment to name and speak out against systems without putting down people. When people stand together, united in this commitment to nonviolence, systemic transformation is possible.

As we seek to enact this kind of transformation, we can benefit from strategies—such as those offered throughout this book—that help us in the countless interactions that are part of living and working together, even while we are still painted with the stain of white supremacy culture. Many of us reading this book already subscribe to a vision of an antiracist community, to the vision of Beloved Community that Dr. King described. Yet despite our longing for this vision, if we don't have workable models and strategies that help us challenge the status quo, we can fail to embody these values as we move through our lives. Without support and new ways of doing things, we will find ourselves taking actions that, upon reflection, reinforce white supremacy's ideas instead of dismantling them. We will find ourselves responding to painful stimuli with harsh judgments that deny the humanity of those whose actions stimulated the harm.

Being from the Global Majority doesn't mean we function outside of white supremacy culture. As we learn to recognize the elements of white supremacy culture that reside inside of us, we gain the power to resist and reroute them. Try to keep these self-reflection questions front and center in your mind:

- Where do I fear there is not enough? What triggers me to start grabbing my share, no matter the cost?
- Where do I choose to blame individuals and communities for how they live and act, rather than recognize the systems that shape and constrain so many of our actions?

- Where do I rush to assuage those in power at the sign of any discomfort? When am I unable to sit with the risk and uncertainty of their distress?

It is by examining our behavior, actions, and beliefs that we are able to take the first steps toward freeing ourselves and returning to choice.

Throughout this book I have shared principles of Nonviolent Communication as a guide to help us navigate difficult moments in ways that align with a commitment to nonviolence and Beloved Community. I have taken the basic principles of Nonviolent Communication and expanded them to include acknowledgment of the systemic. I offer the framework of Authentic Dialogue as one tool we can use in the struggle to dismantle white supremacy culture and practices and other systems of oppression. Through the frame of shared universal human needs, and an expansion into an understanding of the scale of harm brought about by systemic oppression, we can make the compassionate lens through which we view ourselves and others wide enough to take in the way we have all been impacted and harmed. I am not saying that it is easy: working toward Beloved Community requires commitment and perseverance.

Through our immersion in white supremacy culture from birth, our very brains are wired in ways that operate automatically, unquestionably speeding down tracks laid by that culture, to an end that upholds that culture. Compassion is a tool that helps us switch tracks. Compassion for compassionate others is easy, but compassion for those who have done harm is close to impossible unless we are holding an intention for Beloved Community, which guides us through the pain. Learning how to hold ourselves with compassion, even the parts of ourselves that have the capacity to do harm, is the first step to learning how to direct compassion toward those whose actions have had harmful impacts on us. We can work on ourselves first—our self-judgments, our beliefs, and our understanding of what we value—to lay a new path.

All of this lays the foundation for transformative dialogue. The goal of Authentic Dialogue is to enter interactions grounded in commitment to nonviolence and in willingness to show up authentically, while maintaining curiosity about the experience of another—and to return repeatedly to that groundedness and willingness. This is not easy. Author and activist Kazu Haga writes: "If you are not struggling to love people, if you are not trying to build understanding with those you disagree with, then you are not really doing the work of building Beloved Community."[2] It can be excruciatingly difficult and will likely feel impossible at the beginning. It is a huge shift, to go from being self-protective and reactive, to wondering with open-hearted curiosity about the needs that connect you to another.

Even as you enter a dialogue (as grounded as you may think you are!), you may find yourself returning repeatedly to your old patterns. Be kind to yourself, as these are the strategies that your brain created to give your body relief. Thank these strategies for all they have done to protect you in the past, and wish them well as you seek to release them. Each time we fail, we must try to hold ourselves with compassion and resource ourselves in our most supportive relationships. This is because it is through compassion, understanding, and relational support that we can grow the resilience and the new neural pathways that make it possible to try again.

As we near the end of this book, I notice how difficult it feels for me to finish. Endings are challenging for me, and I feel reluctance to say goodbye. So I will leave you with something that I often remind myself. It is true that we may not arrive in Beloved Community in my lifetime, or even in the lifetime of those born after me. It may be generations and generations until the glimmer of Beloved Community shines between us all. But every time I find the courage and self-possession to have an Authentic Dialogue, every time I hold myself with warm compassion, every time I allow myself to pause and recenter toward presence, every time I take action that seeks to meaningfully repair harm, I am laying a paving stone, next to the many others already laid, on the road that will take us there.

NOTES

1. Lillian Roybal Rose, "Healing from Racism: Cross Cultural Leadership Teachings for the Multicultural Future," *Winds of Change* 10, no. 2 (Spring 1995): 14–17.

2. Kazu Haga, *Healing Resistance: A Radically Different Response to Harm. My Life and Training in the Nonviolent Legacy of Dr. King* (Berkeley, CA: Parallax Press, 2020), 106.

APPENDIX

When needs are
met ...

When needs are
unmet ...

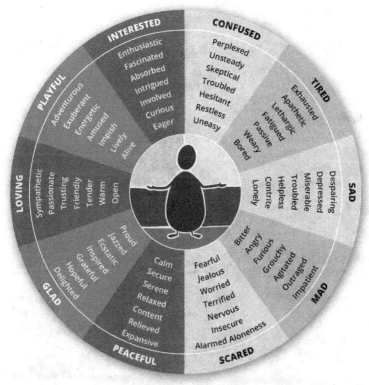

FIGURE 6. Feelings
© Mireille van Bremen and Roxy Manning

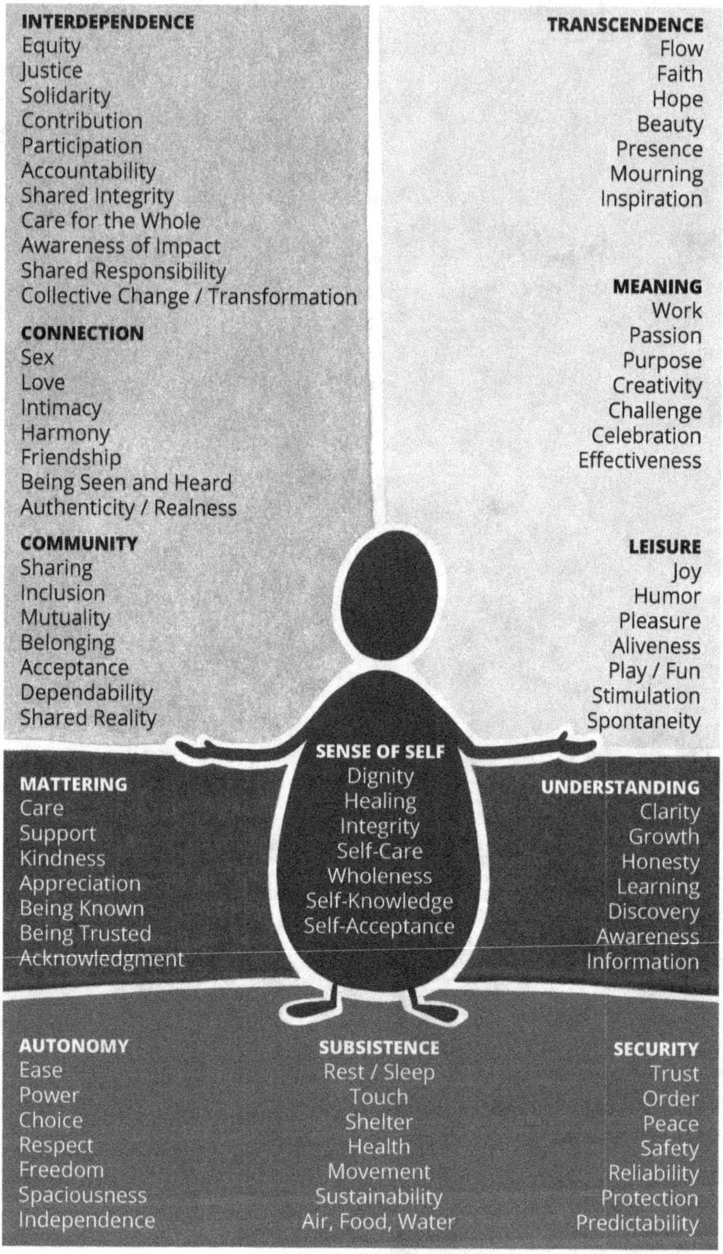

INTERDEPENDENCE
Equity
Justice
Solidarity
Contribution
Participation
Accountability
Shared Integrity
Care for the Whole
Awareness of Impact
Shared Responsibility
Collective Change / Transformation

CONNECTION
Sex
Love
Intimacy
Harmony
Friendship
Being Seen and Heard
Authenticity / Realness

COMMUNITY
Sharing
Inclusion
Mutuality
Belonging
Acceptance
Dependability
Shared Reality

TRANSCENDENCE
Flow
Faith
Hope
Beauty
Presence
Mourning
Inspiration

MEANING
Work
Passion
Purpose
Creativity
Challenge
Celebration
Effectiveness

LEISURE
Joy
Humor
Pleasure
Aliveness
Play / Fun
Stimulation
Spontaneity

SENSE OF SELF
Dignity
Healing
Integrity
Self-Care
Wholeness
Self-Knowledge
Self-Acceptance

MATTERING
Care
Support
Kindness
Appreciation
Being Known
Being Trusted
Acknowledgment

UNDERSTANDING
Clarity
Growth
Honesty
Learning
Discovery
Awareness
Information

AUTONOMY
Ease
Power
Choice
Respect
Freedom
Spaciousness
Independence

SUBSISTENCE
Rest / Sleep
Touch
Shelter
Health
Movement
Sustainability
Air, Food, Water

SECURITY
Trust
Order
Peace
Safety
Reliability
Protection
Predictability

FIGURE 7. **Needs and Values**

© Mireille van Bremen and Roxy Manning

NOTES

Introduction

1. The term Global Majority "includes those people who identify as Black, African, Asian, Brown, Arab and mixed heritage, are indigenous to the global south, and/or have been racialized as 'ethnic minorities.'" Rosemary M. Campbell-Stephens, *Educational Leadership and the Global Majority: Decolonising Narratives* (Cham: Switzerland: Springer Nature, 2021), 7.

2. Quoted in Marjorie Cross Witty, "Marshall Rosenberg," chapter 7 in "Life History Studies of Committed Lives (Volumes I–III)," PhD dissertation, Northwestern University, 1990, pp. 778–779.

3. Quoted in Witty, "Marshall Rosenberg," 785–786.

4. Dominic Barter, "Introduction to Restorative Circles," workshop presented at the New York Intensive in Nonviolent Communication, Albany, NY, August 5, 2008.

5. Campbell-Stephens, *Educational Leadership*, 7.

6. Campbell-Stephens, *Educational Leadership*, 7.

7. Roxy Manning and Sarah Peyton, *The Antiracist Heart: A Self-Compassion and Activism Handbook* (Oakland, CA: Berrett-Koehler, 2023).

Chapter 1

1. Martin Luther King Jr., "Facing the Challenge of a New Age." Address delivered at the First Annual Institute on Nonviolence and Social Change, Martin Luther King Jr. Research and Education Institute, Stanford University, May 24, 2021, https://kinginstitute.stanford.edu

/king-papers/documents/facing-challenge-new-age-address-delivered
-first-annual-institute-nonviolence.

2. Ibram X. Kendi, *Stamped from the Beginning: The Definitive History of Racist Ideas in America* (New York: Bold Type Books, 2017), 124.

3. Kendi, *Stamped from the Beginning,* 508.

4. Marshall B. Rosenberg, *Nonviolent Communication: A Language of Life,* 3rd ed. (Encinitas, CA: PuddleDancer Press, 2015), 178.

Chapter 2

1. Isabel Wilkerson, *Caste: The Origins of Our Discontents* (New York: Random House, 2020), 26.

2. Ibram X. Kendi, *Stamped from the Beginning: The Definitive History of Racist Ideas in America* (New York: Bold Type Books, 2017), 22–46.

3. Kendi, *Stamped from the Beginning,* 22–57.

4. Wes Enzinna, "Inside the Radical, Uncomfortable Movement to Reform White Supremacists," *Mother Jones,* July 11, 2018, https://www .motherjones.com/politics/2018/07/reform-white-supremacists-shane -johnson-life-after-hate/.

5. Kevin Fiscella, "Why Do So Many White Americans Oppose the Affordable Care Act?" *American Journal of Medicine* 129, no. 5 (May 1, 2016), https://doi.org/10.1016/j.amjmed.2015.08.041.

6. German Lopez, "Donald Trump's Long History of Racism, from the 1970s to 2020," *Vox,* updated August 13, 2020, https://www.vox.com /2016/7/25/12270880/donald-trump-racist-racism-history.

7. Rokhaya Diallo, "Opinion | France's Dangerous Move to Remove 'Race' from Its Constitution," *Washington Post,* October 28, 2021, https:// www.washingtonpost.com/news/global-opinions/wp/2018/07/13 /frances-dangerous-move-to-remove-race-from-its-constitution/.

8. Aaryn Urell, "FBI Reports Hate Crimes at Highest Level in 12 Years," Equal Justice Initiative, June 3, 2022, https://eji.org/news/fbi -reports-hate-crimes-at-highest-level-in-12-years/.

9. Linda Darling-Hammond, "Unequal Opportunity: Race and Education," Brookings, July 28, 2016, https://www.brookings.edu/articles /unequal-opportunity-race-and-education/.

10. Tasminda K. Dhaliwal, Mark J. Chin, Virginia S. Lovison, and David M. Quinn, "Educator Bias Is Associated with Racial Disparities in Student Achievement and Discipline," Brookings, March 9, 2022, https://www.brookings.edu/blog/brown-center-chalkboard/2020/07 /20/educator-bias-is-associated-with-racial-disparities-in-student -achievement-and-discipline/.

11. Valerie Strauss, "7 Out of 895—the Number of Black Students Admitted to NYC's Most Selective High School. And There Are More Startling Stats," *Washington Post*, March 21, 2019, https://www.washingtonpost.com/education/2019/03/21/out-number-black-students-admitted-nycs-most-selective-high-school-there-are-more-startling-stats/.

12. Tim Craig, "Florida Legislature Passes Bill That Limits How Schools and Workplaces Teach about Race and Identity," *Washington Post,* March 11, 2022, https://www.washingtonpost.com/nation/2022/03/10/florida-legislature-passes-anti-woke-bill/. Manny Diaz, "Florida Senate—2022 SB 148," Calendar for 11/27/2022—The Florida Senate, https://www.flsenate.gov/Session/Bill/2022/148/BillText/Filed/HTML (accessed November 27, 2022), lines 71–72.

13. Myisha V. Cherry, "Breaking Racial Rules through Rage," Reynolds Lecture, Learning On Demand, Elon University, April 2019, https://blogs.elon.edu/ondemand/breaking-racial-rules-through-rage-myisha-cherry/ (accessed November 27, 2022).

14. James Baldwin, "As Much Truth as One Can Bear," *New York Times Book Review*, January 14, 1962, p. 38, https://nyti.ms/3imS51K.

Chapter 3

1. Martin Luther King Jr., " 'When Peace Becomes Obnoxious'," Martin Luther King Jr. Research and Education Institute, Stanford University, May 24, 2021, https://kinginstitute.stanford.edu/king-papers/documents/when-peace-becomes-obnoxious.

2. King, " 'When Peace Becomes Obnoxious'."

3. Marshall B. Rosenberg, *Nonviolent Communication: A Language of Life,* 3rd ed. (Encinitas, CA: PuddleDancer Press, 2015), 16.

4. "FNS—Elder Teachings by Napos," University of Wisconsin-Green Bay, February 28, 2011, https://youtu.be/LK5Et8MJJJA. "Medicine Ways: Traditional Healers and Healing," U.S. National Library of Medicine, National Institutes of Health, https://www.nlm.nih.gov/nativevoices/exhibition/healing-ways/medicine-ways/medicine-wheel.html (accessed October 2022).

Chapter 4

1. "Understanding Unconscious Bias," *Shortwave,* NPR, aired July 15, 2020, https://www.npr.org/2020/07/14/891140598/understanding-unconscious-bias.

2. Carol C. Mukhopadhyay, Rosemary Henze, and Yolanda T. Moses, *How Real Is Race?: A Sourcebook on Race, Culture, and Biology*, 2nd ed. (Lanham, MD: Rowman & Littlefield Publishers, 2013). A great exploration on the invention of race is Christine Herbes-Sommers, Tracy Heather Strain, and Llewellyn Smith, dirs., *Race: The Power of an Illusion* (San Francisco, CA: California Newsreel, 2003), https://www.racepowerofanillusion.org/.

3. Stephan Lewandowsky, Ullrich K. Ecker, Colleen M. Seifert, Norbert Schwarz, and John Cook, "Misinformation and Its Correction: Continued Influence and Successful Debiasing," *Psychological Science in the Public Interest* 13, no. 3 (September 17, 2012): 106–31, https://doi.org/10.1177/1529100612451018.

4. Fredrick C. Harris, "The Rise of Respectability Politics," *Dissent Magazine* (Winter 2014), https://www.dissentmagazine.org/article/the-rise-of-respectability-politics.

5. Harris, "Rise of Respectability Politics."

6. Shai Davidai and Thomas Gilovich, "The Headwinds/Tailwinds Asymmetry: An Availability Bias in Assessments of Barriers and Blessings," *Journal of Personality and Social Psychology* 111, no. 6 (2016): 835–51, https://doi.org/10.1037/pspa0000066.

7. Jessica Nordell, *The End of Bias: A Beginning: The Science and Practice of Overcoming Unconscious Bias* (New York: Metropolitan Books, 2021).

Chapter 6

1. Bryan Hancock, James Manyika, Monne Williams, and Lareina Yee, "The Black Experience at Work in Charts," *McKinsey Quarterly* (December 13, 2021), https://www.mckinsey.com/featured-insights/diversity-and-inclusion/the-black-experience-at-work-in-charts.

2. Inbal Kashtan and Miki Kashtan, "Connection Requests: Motivations and Examples," in *2014 BayNVC Nonviolent Communication Leadership Program* (Oakland, CA: BayNVC, 2014), 31–34.

Chapter 7

1. Erica Sherover-Marcuse, "Liberation Theory: A Working Framework," Radical Resilience Institute, p. 1, https://drive.google.com/file/d/1nzMWyo5htEODgHiTy5knF3oiGdKU5xA7/view (accessed September 15, 2022).

2. "The King Philosophy—Nonviolence365®," Martin Luther King

Jr. Center for Nonviolent Social Change, February 25, 2022, https://thekingcenter.org/about-tkc/the-king-philosophy/.

3. Aelita Kapitonovna (Dawna) Markova, *I Will Not Die an Unlived Life: Reclaiming Purpose and Passion* (Berkeley, CA: Conari Press, 2000), 2.

Chapter 8

1. Monnica T. Williams, "Microaggressions: Clarification, Evidence, and Impact," *Perspectives on Psychological Science* 15, no. 1 (2019): 3–26, https://doi.org/10.1177/1745691619827499. Derald Wing Sue et al., "Racial Microaggressions in Everyday Life: Implications for Clinical Practice," *American Psychologist* 62, no. 4 (2007): 271–286.

2. Lisa B. Spanierman, D. Anthony Clark, and Yeeun Kim, "Reviewing Racial Microaggressions Research: Documenting Targets' Experiences, Harmful Sequelae, and Resistance Strategies," *Perspectives on Psychological Science* 16, no. 5 (2021): 1037–1059.

3. Spanierman, Clark, and Kim, "Reviewing Racial Microaggressions Research."

4. Isabel Wilkerson, *Caste: The Origins of Our Discontents* (New York: Random House, 2020).

5. Williams, "Microaggressions," 4.

Chapter 10

1. Lillian Roybal Rose, "Healing from Racism: Cross Cultural Leadership Teachings for the Multicultural Future," *Winds of Change* 10, no. 2 (Spring 1995): 14–17.

2. Kazu Haga, *Healing Resistance: A Radically Different Response to Harm. My Life and Training in the Nonviolent Legacy of Dr. King* (Berkeley, CA: Parallax Press, 2020), 106.

ACKNOWLEDGMENTS

If you read this far, you understand why this book feels like a miracle. I wish I could go back to that nineteen-year-old who had dreamed of being a writer and tell her it would be okay, that the community who will surround her with love and support is stronger than anyone who tries to tear her down. I wish I could tell her that there are so many people who will show up in unexpected ways—to tell her "we see you, we believe in you"—that there won't be enough space to thank them all. But here, I want to thank just a few.

I'll start with someone I won't name but who will recognize themself. When the proposal was turned down by the head of one publishing company, the editor tasked with reviewing the book wrote me personally. In that moment when I wanted to give up, reading of their belief that this book will help bring these concepts mainstream, and their offer to help in any way they could, gave me hope to try again. Thank you.

Ryan Honeyman—for believing in my work and, as soon as you heard of my first rejection, saying: "I have an editor. I'll send him a message right now!" You made this possible.

Neal Maillet—for your delight at this book proposal and

patient responses to numerous questions. For sharing the places where these books took you and advocating to bring them to life. For responding with compassion and understanding to life's unfolding. And to all the BK staff for their excitement, expertise, and support in bringing this book (and the handbook!) to print.

Mireille van Bremen—thank you for taking rambling conversations and bringing them to life, for endless revisions, and celebrating feedback, for check-ins and honoring grief, for balancing life and working at a sustainable pace. The images in this book surpassed my dreams.

When I started writing, I spent more than a month staring at my computer, frozen. Who was I to think I had anything to share? As I struggled with fear, my Tower Team gathered around me. "Let's meet weekly," they said. We began with long video calls: "Just talk to us. What's the book about? What are you thinking of these days?" They empathized when my self-judgment was strong and shared my delight when the words flowed. As the book progressed, they lent their expertise—reviewing drafts, making suggestions, sharing their stories, volunteering in roleplays. The most remarkable part is that each time I called a Tower, a different mix of folks would show up, saying yes only when it truly served them. It healed my story of being too needy, of having to go it alone, with their caring support. Thank you to Alicia Garcia, David Johnson, David Pursell, Donna Carter, Edmundo Norte, Janey Skinner, Kristin Masters, Mike Tinoco, Ranjana Ariaratnam, Shannon Casey, Susan Strasburger, and Talli Jackson.

Along with my Tower Team, several people jumped in and lifted me up along the way. Jessica Schaffer and Sandra Thomson jumped in with thoughtful feedback. Early readers

Miki Kashtan and Karen DeGannes paused their busy lives and did a meticulous read of each chapter, providing hours of constructive feedback that improved this book, conveyed on a vehicle of love. Having people I admire as much as them find value in this work thrills me to no end.

Gwendolyn Wilson, Kit Miller, Kathy Simon, Marc Scruggs, and Noel Legoburu were excited before they even opened the draft manuscript. Their utter faith that this would be worth reading, and their enthusiastic words of resonance, healing, and hope buoyed me over these final stretches.

Marc Scruggs, Paul Merritt, Gail Caroll, and Kathleen Macferran—I'm so grateful for your contributions to help the message of this book spread far and wide. I hope our collective dream of this work ending in many hands and contributing to change in our world comes true.

Alejandra Delgado, also part of my Tower Team, was my rock in so many ways. A trusted friend and colleague, she introduced me to new thinkers and brought a nuanced eye to editing that caught so many things I missed the first and second time around. And in addition, she picked up all the family and work responsibilities I dropped—countless grocery runs, meals, late-night empathy. Her encouragement of my self-care made this process one I'm leaving stronger than when I started.

Ranjana Ariaratnam, David Johnson, and Lakshmi Ariaratnam—I can truly say this book would not exist without you. David and Ranji—I think at this point, given the number of close reads and hands-on manipulation of this book, you know it better than I do. The level of trust I have in your work is indescribable. Just knowing that any task you take on will be done more thoroughly than I could have imagined, and more accurately than I could have hoped for, made this process possible. You embody total acceptance, love, and incredible brilliance. In the middle of one of the hardest periods of my life, you helped me see the power of ritual and self-care, interdependence and nurturing, generosity and love. And of course, Bananagrams to revive. Drink more water!

Mom and Dad, Lois and Milton Manning—you modeled what it means to persist against white supremacy ideology, to take risks when speaking up against injustice, and working to help even the most vulnerable people be held with care. Your love made this possible.

Anika and Theo—thank you for laughter and your hugs. For standing up for the things you value and cherishing connection and care. For giving me hope that each generation is a little further down the path of Beloved Community. You are the ones I've been waiting for. Micah—above all, this book is for you.

INDEX

ABOUT THE AUTHOR

ROXY MANNING, PhD, clinical psychologist and Certified Trainer of Nonviolent Communication, brings decades of service experience to her work interrupting explicitly and implicitly oppressive attitudes and cultural norms. Roxy has worked, consulted, and provided training across the United States with businesses, nonprofits, and government organizations wanting to move toward equitable and diverse workplace cultures, as well as internationally in over ten countries with individuals and groups committed to social justice. As a psychologist, she works in San Francisco serving the homeless and disenfranchised mentally ill population. Roxy is also the coauthor with Sarah Peyton of the companion text, *The Antiracist Heart: A Self-Compassion and Activism Handbook*.

Berrett–Koehler
BK Publishers

Berrett-Koehler is an independent publisher dedicated to an ambitious mission: *Connecting people and ideas to create a world that works for all.*

Our publications span many formats, including print, digital, audio, and video. We also offer online resources, training, and gatherings. And we will continue expanding our products and services to advance our mission.

We believe that the solutions to the world's problems will come from all of us, working at all levels: in our society, in our organizations, and in our own lives. Our publications and resources offer pathways to creating a more just, equitable, and sustainable society. They help people make their organizations more humane, democratic, diverse, and effective (and we don't think there's any contradiction there). And they guide people in creating positive change in their own lives and aligning their personal practices with their aspirations for a better world.

And we strive to practice what we preach through what we call "The BK Way." At the core of this approach is *stewardship,* a deep sense of responsibility to administer the company for the benefit of all of our stakeholder groups, including authors, customers, employees, investors, service providers, sales partners, and the communities and environment around us. Everything we do is built around stewardship and our other core values of *quality, partnership, inclusion,* and *sustainability.*

This is why Berrett-Koehler is the first book publishing company to be both a B Corporation (a rigorous certification) and a benefit corporation (a for-profit legal status), which together require us to adhere to the highest standards for corporate, social, and environmental performance. And it is why we have instituted many pioneering practices (which you can learn about at www.bkconnection.com), including the Berrett-Koehler Constitution, the Bill of Rights and Responsibilities for BK Authors, and our unique Author Days.

We are grateful to our readers, authors, and other friends who are supporting our mission. We ask you to share with us examples of how BK publications and resources are making a difference in your lives, organizations, and communities at www.bkconnection.com/impact.

Dear reader,

Thank you for picking up this book and welcome to the worldwide BK community! You're joining a special group of people who have come together to create positive change in their lives, organizations, and communities.

What's BK all about?

Our mission is to connect people and ideas to create a world that works for all.

Why? Our communities, organizations, and lives get bogged down by old paradigms of self-interest, exclusion, hierarchy, and privilege. But we believe that can change. That's why we seek the leading experts on these challenges—and share their actionable ideas with you.

A welcome gift

To help you get started, we'd like to offer you a **free copy** of one of our bestselling ebooks:

www.bkconnection.com/welcome

When you claim your **free ebook**, you'll also be subscribed to our blog.

Our freshest insights

Access the best new tools and ideas for leaders at all levels on our blog at ideas.bkconnection.com.

Sincerely,

Your friends at Berrett-Koehler

Certified

Corporation